POETS ON PROZAC

Poets on Prozac

MENTAL ILLNESS, TREATMENT, *and the* CREATIVE PROCESS

Edited by

RICHARD M. BERLIN, MD

ASSOCIATE PROFESSOR OF PSYCHIATRY

UNIVERSITY OF MASSACHUSETTS

MEDICAL SCHOOL

WORCESTER, MASSACHUSETTS

The Johns Hopkins University Press

BALTIMORE

© 2008 The Johns Hopkins University Press
All rights reserved. Published 2008
Printed in the United States of America on acid-free paper
9 8 7 6 5 4 3 2 1

The Johns Hopkins University Press
2715 North Charles Street
Baltimore, Maryland 21218-4363
www.press.jhu.edu

Library of Congress Cataloging-in-Publication Data

Poets on Prozac: mental illness, treatment, and the creative
process / edited by Richard M. Berlin.
    p.   ;   cm.
Includes bibliographical references.
ISBN-13: 978-0-8018-8839-7 (hardcover : alk. paper)
ISBN-10: 0-8018-8839-5 (hardcover : alk. paper)
1. Artists—Mental health—Case studies. 2. Mental illness—
Treatment—Case studies. 3. Psychotherapy—Case studies.
4. Personality and creative ability. 5. Creation (Literary, artistic, etc.)
6. Creative ability. 7. Art and mental illness. I. Berlin, Richard M.
[DNLM: 1. Mental Disorders—drug therapy—Personal Narratives.
2. Mental Disorders—psychology—Personal Narratives.
3. Creativeness—Personal Narratives. 4. Poetry—Personal
Narratives.   WM 402 P743 2008]
RC451.4.A7P54 2008
616.89—dc22   2007037384

A catalog record for this book is available from the British Library.

Special discounts are available for bulk purchases of this book.
For more information, please contact Special Sales at 410-516-6936
or specialsales@jhu.edu.

The Johns Hopkins University Press uses environmentally friendly
book materials, including recycled text paper that is composed of
at least 30 percent post-consumer waste, whenever possible.
All of our book papers are acid-free, and our jackets and
covers are printed on paper with recycled content.

For Susanne

CONTENTS

RENÉE ASHLEY, MA, is the author of three volumes of poetry: *Salt* (Brittingham Prize in Poetry), *The Various Reasons of Light*, *The Revisionist's Dream*, and a chapbook, *The Museum of Lost Wings*, as well as a novel, *Someplace Like This*. She has received fellowships from the New Jersey State Council on the Arts and the National Endowment for the Arts. A contributing editor to the *Literary Review*, she is on the faculty of Fairleigh Dickinson University's low-residency MFA Program in Creative Writing.

The latest two books of poems by DAVID BUDBILL, MDiv, are *While We've Still Got Feet* (2005) and *Moment to Moment: Poems of a Mountain Recluse* (1999). Boxholder Records released *Songs for a Suffering World: A Prayer for Peace, a Protest against War*, with bassist William Parker and drummer Hamid Drake in 2003, and *Zen Mountains–Zen Streets: A Duet for Poet and Improvised Bass*, with the music of William Parker, in 1999. Also in 1999, Chelsea Green Publishing Company republished a revised, expanded version of *Judevine*, Budbill's collected poems.

JACK COULEHAN, MD, is a professor of medicine and preventive medicine at Stony Brook University, where he directs the medical humanities and bioethics program. He has published four collections of poetry, most recently *Medicine Stone* (2002), and written or edited several other books, notably *The Medical Interview: Mastering Skills for Clinical Practice* (5th ed., 2006) and *Primary Care: More Poems by Physicians* (2006). Coulehan's honors and awards include National Endowment for the Humanities and Pennsylvania Council on the Arts fellowships, the American College of Physicians Award for Poetry, the American

Nurses' Association Book Award, the Merck Award at Yaddo, and the American Academy of Hospice and Palliative Medicine Humanities Award.

The most recent books by DENISE DUHAMEL, MFA, are *Two and Two* (2005), *Mille et un sentiments* (2005), and *Queen for a Day: Selected and New Poems* (2001). Her work has been anthologized widely, including in six editions of *Best American Poetry*. A recipient of a fellowship from the National Endowment for the Arts, she teaches creative writing at Florida International University in Miami.

Living in Jacksonville, Florida, CATERINA EPPOLITO, MA, MFA, is a poet and licensed psychotherapist who earned a Herbert Fellowship in creative writing from the University of Florida and was a professor of clinical psychology at St. Michael's College, Vermont. She was a semifinalist in the *Nation*'s poetry contest, and in the following year her poem "Bedlam Nursery Rhyme" appeared in the *Nation*. She is working on a book about eating disorders entitled *Through the Looking Glass and Back*.

Poems by VANESSA HALEY, MFA, MSW, have appeared in *Reading Poetry: An Anthology of Poems* (1988) and in literary journals such as *Poetry*, the *Gettysburg Review*, the *Alaska Quarterly Review*, and *Southern Poetry Review*. Robert Pinsky recently selected one of her poems for the 2006 Poetry Prize *(Dogwood: A Journal of Poetry and Prose)*, and she was the first recipient of the John Haines Poetry Award from *Ice-Floe: International Poetry of the Far North* (2001). Her book of poems, *The Logic of Wings* (http://www.cherry-grove.com/haley.html), was published ten years after she left a tenured associate professorship in English to become a psychotherapist.

ANDREW HUDGINS, MFA, is Humanities Distinguished Professor in English at Ohio State University. He has published six books of poetry and one book of literary criticism, and his essays have appeared in the *American Scholar*, the *Washington Post Magazine*, the *Hudson Review*, and many others. He was recently made a member of the Fellowship of Southern Writers.

THOMAS KRAMPF is the author of four collections of poetry. He has read his work both nationally and internationally, including on National Public Radio and at the 2006 Printemps des Poetes festival in La

Rochelle, France, with leading poets from France and Iran. His fifth book, *Poems to My Wife and Other Women,* is scheduled for publication in fall 2007.

BARBARA F. LEFCOWITZ, PhD, has published nine books of poetry as well as poems, stories, and more than five hundred essays in journals. She has won fellowships from the National Endowment for the Humanities, the National Endowment for the Arts, and the Rockefeller Foundation, among others. Also a visual artist, she lives in Bethesda, Maryland.

GWYNETH LEWIS, DPhil, was the first National Poet of Wales. An award-winning poet, she has published six books of poetry in both Welsh and English and two books of nonfiction, *Sunbathing in the Rain: A Cheerful Book on Depression* (2002) and *Two in a Boat: The True Story of a Marital Rite of Passage* (2005). She has written three libretti for Welsh National Opera and is a Fellow of the Royal Society of Literature.

JESSE MILLNER, MFA, teaches composition and creative writing at Florida Gulf Coast University. His first book of poetry, *The Drowned Boys,* was published in 2005. His most recent book, *On the Saturday after the Rapture,* was released in 2006.

LIZA PORTER'S essay "In Plainview" (2005) was listed as a notable essay in *Best American Essays 2006.* Other work has appeared in the anthology *What Wildness Is This: Women Write about the Southwest* (2007), *AGNI, Barrow Street, Hotel Amerika, Diner,* and other magazines. She is director of the Other Voices Women's Reading Series in Tucson, Arizona.

REN POWELL, MA, is the author of two books of poetry, the most recent entitled *Mixed States* (2004). She has published nine books of translations, and her own poetry has been translated into Norwegian, French, Spanish, Croatian, and Basque. Powell's dramatic works have been performed in the United States, Canada, and Norway.

MARTHA SILANO, MFA, is the author of two book-length collections, *Blue Positive* (2006) and *What the Truth Tastes Like* (1999). Her work has also appeared in the *Paris Review, Prairie Schooner,* and *TriQuarterly,* among others. Silano teaches at Bellevue and Edmonds Community Colleges.

J. D. SMITH, MA, was awarded a 2007 Fellowship in Poetry from the National Endowment for the Arts. He has published two collections of poetry, *The Hypothetical Landscape* and *Settling for Beauty*, and a children's book, *The Best Mariachi in the World*. He lives and works in Washington, DC.

CHASE TWICHELL, MFA, is the author of six books of poetry (most recently *Dog Language* (2006), as well as a translation (with Tony Stewart) of *Tagore: The Lover of God* (2003), and co-editor of *The Practice of Poetry: Writing Exercises from Poets Who Teach*. She has taught at Hampshire College, Warren Wilson College, Goddard College, the University of Alabama, and Princeton University. In 1999 she left academia to start Ausable Press, which publishes contemporary poetry.

ACKNOWLEDGMENTS

This project began with a misunderstanding. Paul Genova, MD, a fellow columnist at *Psychiatric Times,* invited me to write a piece on poetry and psychiatry. I readily agreed, only to discover that Paul was inviting me to write an entire book. When I declined, telling Paul I wanted to spend my time writing poetry rather than writing about poetry, his reply was, "Write a book on whatever you want in psychiatry! I'll see if I can make it happen!" Over a glass or two of wine, I brainstormed with my wife, Susanne King, MD, an avid reader and a child/adolescent psychiatrist. We came up with the idea that evolved into the current volume. Unfortunately, Paul's situation changed, and we could not complete the project together. But I was excited by the idea of the book and forged ahead.

Jeff Herman, literary agent, confirmed the potential audience for the book and provided excellent advice and encouragement. My psychiatrist-poet/psychologist-poet friends Ron Pies, MD, Paul Fleishman, MD, and Robert Deluty, PhD, also provided the support I needed to carry the book to the finish line. Albert Rothenberg, MD, reviewed my introduction and made excellent suggestions, which enhanced the final version. I would also like to thank Leo Cristofar, managing editor, and Ron Pies, MD, editor-in-chief of *Psychiatric Times,* for continuing to publish my poems each month in "Poetry of the *Times.*" Wendy Harris, medical editor at the Johns Hopkins University Press, has maintained a wonderful balance of enthusiasm, wisdom, experience, and clear structure.

Finally, I would like to thank the poets who wrote the essays for this book. They have handled the process of writing, editing, and revision with professional grace, and I continue to feel a sense of awe and humility each time I read their essays. This is their book. Their resilience reminds me of the importance of effective treatment for my patients, and their creativity inspires me to do my best as a doctor and as a poet.

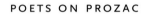

POETS ON PROZAC

RICHARD M. BERLIN, MD

*Poets are damned but they are not blind, they see with the
eyes of angels.* —WILLIAM CARLOS WILLIAMS

Everywhere I go I find that a poet has been there before me.
—SIGMUND FREUD

THROUGHOUT MY CAREER as a psychiatrist, I have treated creative people from many disciplines—poets, writers, artists, professors, scientists, entrepreneurs—and have been privileged to witness the growth in creativity that accompanied effective treatment. Yet as I shared my patients' satisfaction with their progress, I wondered how psychotherapy, psychoactive medications, and other forms of psychiatric treatment might free us to work at our highest creative levels. This collection of essays allows creative people—in this case, poets—to reveal the inner workings of how psychiatric treatment affected their creativity.

Because creativity is not limited to poets, the reader may ask why I have focused my inquiry on this highly select group. My reasoning is simple: in addition to my work as a physician, I am also a poet, and I know from experience that poets are among the most fearless of writers when it comes to self-revelation. In this collection of essays, a number of our finest contemporary poets write about their experiences with psychiatric treatment.

To be considered as essayists for this book, poets had to demonstrate a high level of creativity based on publication of at least one book of poetry as well as a publication in literary journals. My strategy for finding poet-essayists began with scanning my bookshelf and writing to all the poets whose work I love. My cover letter explained that I had no idea about whether they had ever received any type of psychiatric treatment (though there was an occasional exception, when I knew the psychiatric history from a poet's published work). I asked the poets for an essay that would explore the influence of psychiatric treatment on their creative process, including examples of poems that would give the reader a sense of how their poetry had changed after treatment. I also ran two advertisements in *Poets and Writers* magazine. In addition, poets contacted me after learning about the project from other contributors. About one-third of the essays came from each of the three groups.

The essays address many of the key questions about psychiatric treatment and creativity. Do poets need to be mentally ill to produce great work? Does mental illness enhance or diminish creativity? What is the influence of substance use/abuse? What are the benefits and risks of prescribed psychoactive medications? Is creativity heightened by treatment, or does treatment reduce emotional pain to the extent that the poet no longer has anything to say? Does a person have to be "crazy" to write good poetry? What do poets themselves define as crucial elements in their creative process?

Poets are also an obvious group to ask about psychiatric treatment because, as a group, poets may have a high incidence of psychiatric disorders. Popular culture has reinforced this idea: Shakespeare wrote, "The lunatic, the lover, and the poet are of one imagination all compact," and Robert Burton was even more direct when he wrote, "All poets are mad." In our own era, depression in poets has been called "the Sylvia Plath effect," named for the poet who committed suicide when she was thirty-one years old. Current psychiatric research suggests that poets have a high rate of depression and suicide. In a study of thirty poets at the prestigious Iowa Writer's Workshop, Nancy Andreasen, MD, the former editor of the *American Journal of Psychiatry*, reported that 80 percent had a mood disorder. Poets also tend to die at a younger age than other writers: sixty-two years for poets; sixty-eight years for nonfiction writers. An entire generation of poets, including Plath, Anne Sexton, Robert Lowell, and Dylan Thomas, became famous for the dramatic excesses of their psychiatric disorders and substance abuse. I have often wondered whether our current treatment options would have altered the lives of these poets and enhanced their work and also whether some poets avoided any psychiatric treatment, fearing that treatment might have deleterious effects on their creativity.

For example, consider poet-physician William Carlos Williams's assessment of the psychiatric care he received fifty years ago when he became depressed following a stroke. At that time, psychoanalytic psychotherapy (described by one of Freud's early patients as "the talking cure") was the dominant treatment method:

Have you ever been in the hands of a psychiatrist? My advice is, stay away. They reverse the usual medical process to which the whole profession has accustomed itself since the beginning of time. They present to the patient not a sympathetic ear, but a cold front. It isn't pleasant. I am going through a depressed phase following a stroke last August and undergoing a course in their specialty. I might as well be experiencing treatment by a frog! I don't like it. Oh, for the kind heart of an old-fashioned country doctor! Poets have always been among the unfortunates of the world.[1]

Fortunately, psychiatric treatment strategies have improved since Williams's era. Current standards of practice require a thorough diagnostic assessment and discussion with the patient about an array of treatment options, including psychotherapy, medication, or a combination of treatment interventions. When medication is prescribed, the psychiatrist and patient must work together to find the most effective drug and pay close attention to adjusting the dosage to provide the maximum benefit with the fewest side effects. Even with our advances in psychiatric treatment, I must acknowledge the tension that exists between our culture's attitude toward creativity, which is always extraordinarily positive, and its more ambivalent assessment of psychiatric treatment, which has both risks and benefits. At the negative extreme, psychiatrists, psychiatric treatment, and psychiatric patients (referred to by antipsychiatry groups as "psychiatric survivors") can evoke images of dilapidated state hospitals, totalitarian mind control, and crude interventions, such as electroconvulsive therapy delivered without anesthesia or prefontal lobotomy. Psychiatric treatment has rarely (if ever) been portrayed accurately in movies, with psychiatrists depicted as either an ineffectual "Dr. Dippy" or a sadistic "Dr. Evil."[2] Many insurance companies (and state laws) have discriminatory coverage that limits the benefits paid for treatment of psychiatric disorders as compared to other medical disorders. These restrictions lead to a situation in some parts of our country in which highly skilled psychiatrists and psychotherapists simply can't be found.

On the positive side of the ambivalence toward psychiatric treatment are new psychoactive medications like the selective serotonin reuptake inhibitors (SSRIs), of which Prozac is the most famous. The SSRIs are currently in the top ten of all medications prescribed in the

United States. SSRIs, which are safer, more easily tolerated drugs than the previous generation of antidepressant medications, treat both depression and anxiety effectively and make some people feel "better than well." Peter D. Kramer, MD, described these effects in his best-selling book *Listening to Prozac* (1993) and coined the term *cosmetic psychopharmacology* to address his finding that some of his patients felt like their "actual self" or "true self" only when treated with an SSRI, perhaps due to the lifting of lifelong feelings of depression. Some medical ethicists have grouped Prozac with other "enhancement technologies," like botox or plastic surgery, medical interventions that do not treat a disease but enhance wellness.[3] If psychiatric medications can alter a poet's sense of his or her authentic self, reduce the sense of alienation, depression, melancholy, or angst, can the poet continue to be creative, and if so, how will his or her poetry change? How would contemporary poets respond to the famous statement of the great German poet Ranier Maria Rilke: "If I lose my demons, I will lose my angels as well." This is a crucial issue many of the poet-essayists will explore.

There is now strong evidence that mental illness impedes the creative process. As medication treatment has become safer and more acceptable to patients, psychiatrists have shifted their theories about mental disorders from a psychoanalytic model to a broader view that incorporates the idea that serious mental disorders such as depression, manic-depressive illness, schizophrenia, obsessive-compulsive disorder, anxiety disorders, and substance dependence are biologically based disorders resulting (in popular terms) from "chemical imbalances" in the brain. When patients are acutely ill, these psychiatric disorders block creativity. Severe depression interferes with motivation, energy, drive, realistic self-assessment, and pleasure. (Sylvia Plath wrote, "When you are insane, you are busy being insane—all the time. . . . When I was crazy, that's all I was.")[4] Severe anxiety inhibits performance (just look at the prescription sales of Viagra if you need to be convinced about the effects of performance anxiety). The disorganization of thinking, including hallucinations and delusions, in people with schizophrenia or manic-depressive illness during a period of active psychosis also stifles creativity. And writers who experiment with drugs and alcohol or become addicted to them most often obtain *a feeling* of enhanced creativity rather than producing creative work that is highly valued by others. Writers like Hemingway and Fitzgerald may have done their best work in their twenties and thirties before their lives and creativity had been damaged by alcohol.

On the other hand, there is also evidence that some forms of mental illness may enhance, or at least coexist with creativity. Kay Redfield Jamison described an overlap between manic-depressive illness and "the artistic temperament." In an appendix to her classic book *Touched with Fire* (1993), Jamison presents an extraordinary list of poets, writers, composers, visual artists, and musicians who she believes were likely to have had manic-depressive illness or one of its subtypes. Jamison believes that the common view of the artistic temperament—a person with tremendous energy, expansive mood, intelligence, and grand vision alternating with darker moods and bouts of "madness," brooding, and volatility—fits closely with the behavioral characteristics of people with manic-depressive illness. (Because all the artists Jamison describes are dead, her assessment is based on historical evidence rather than direct clinical evaluation.) Jamison's assertion leads us to the question of how to define creativity and encourages us to explore the actual research that supports or challenges our stereotypes of poets and the creative process.

Alice Flaherty, a neurologist, creativity researcher, and author of the brilliant book *The Midnight Disease* (2004), believes creative acts must combine novelty and value. Novelty is required because customary solutions are not creative, even if they are ingenious and useful. Creative works must be valuable because a work that is merely odd is not creative. Unusual but valueless behavior, which may occur in people with severe mental disorders, shares a border with creativity but does not fit this definition. Of course, any definition of creativity is strongly influenced by our idea that everyone has a wellspring of creativity and can be creative in their daily lives—in their work, hobbies, and relationships. Where we draw the line between these activities and the productions of highly creative people is arbitrary. Flaherty also points out that creativity occurs in a social context: different generations may have vastly different assessments of a writer's work.

Another leader in the field of creativity research is Albert Rothenberg, MD, whose book *Creativity and Madness* (1990) summarizes his thirty-five years of research as the principal investigator for the project "Studies on the Creative Process." In the course of his research, Rothenberg and associates performed controlled studies based on the assessment of the mental processes of highly creative people, including Nobel Laureates, Pulitzer Prize winners, poet laureates, and winners of the Bollingen Poetry Prize. Rothenberg himself had previously interviewed the highly creative individuals directly and reviewed their notes and manuscripts in progress with them to understand their creative process. One of Rothenberg's main findings is startling: "Only one characteristic of personality and orientation to life and work is ab-solutely, *across the board,* present in *all* creative people: motivation."[5]

Although our cultural stereotype is that great ideas suddenly appear in the minds of creative people without effort, the creative process, in Rothenberg's view, actually results from "direct, intense, and inten-tional effort on the creator's part."[6] In the process of creativity, people are constantly looking for new ideas, approaches, and solutions. Roth-enberg found that inspiration only becomes creation after an enor-mous amount of work and preparation, and the artist or scientist must be motivated specifically to create. As Thomas Edison put it so fa-mously, "Genius is one percent inspiration and ninety-nine percent perspiration."

In contrast to Jamison's assertion about "the artistic temperament," Rothenberg was unable to find a specific personality type associated with outstanding creativity; his subjects were no more childish, eccen-tric, erratic, rebellious, egotistical, or impulsive than other groups. In-terestingly, many had a style that was somewhat rigid, meticulous, and perfectionistic rather than the free and spontaneous style we often as-sociate with the stereotype of creative artists. He reported that, based on IQ testing, highly creative people in literature and the arts were not all exceptionally intelligent.

Rothenberg's data stand in contrast to what he calls the "myths of creativity"—myths, because none has been empirically assessed or substantiated:

Myth 1: The Myth of Inspiration. This myth is typified by the story of the poet who writes a poem directly from his or her head as if taking dictation from God, or the story of a composer who suddenly hears an entire symphony in his or her mind and merely transcribes the notes. This myth is often connected with a sense of strangeness and madness and dates back to the ancient Greeks, who believed that passion, not in-telligence, was the source of creativity: poets received their ideas in a frenzy at moments when they were possessed by the Muse. During the Renaissance, melancholy became linked to creativity, and the nine-teenth-century Romantics amplified this idea.

Rothenberg believes creative people themselves have perpetuated the myth of inspiration because creativity is so highly valued. One might say that this myth is a marketing strategy for poets, who earn very little money from writing, are often unrecognized, and need a mystique to bolster their self-esteem. Data derived from a study of poets' manuscripts by Phyllis Bartlett show that inspiration was not a key element in their creative process. In reviewing poems from the first draft to the final, published poem, Bartlett found that the poetic process consisted of intense work and revision. Starting a poem was not generally greeted by the poet with a sense of inspiration, breakthrough, or relief; the early draft actually created a degree of tension the poet tried to resolve by discovering "what the poem [was] really trying to say."[7]

Myth 2: The Myth of Very Special Talent. This myth suggests that a special talent can be observed in the childhood of all great artists. The special talent may be an "eidetic" faculty, such as having perfect visual memory, or being able to interchange one sensory faculty for another, like converting visual images directly into music. However, there is no evidence that these processes actually take place in anyone. And, as noted earlier, with a few exceptions in science and music, there is little evidence that extraordinarily high intelligence is required for creativity. Rothenberg did find that highly creative people typically had at least one parent who was healthy psychologically and one parent who was interested, or had tried and not succeeded, in a particular creative field. He concluded that "the creative person . . . strives to fulfill a parent's *implicit, unrealized* yearnings."[8]

One additional notion of creativity, which has been derived from Freud's psychoanlytic formulations, is that creativity resides in "the unconscious" and that creative work is a way to convert unconscious conflict into a more acceptable form in order to reduce anxiety. Freud also drew a distinction between what he called primary-process thinking, which occurs in psychosis and dreams, and secondary-process thinking, which is more logical and is language-based. In this view, creativity results from a balance between primary-process and secondary-process thinking. Jackson Pollock, who spent a year in Jungian analysis and created his "psychoanalytic drawings," supported the psychoanalytic formulation when he declared, "The source of my painting is the unconscious."

Researchers like Flaherty have helped us begin to understand the neurological underpinnings of creativity. In a theory that parallels the primary-process/secondary-process model, Flaherty has begun to view the the brain as a "poetry-making organ." Although popular culture attributes creative thinking to the right side of the brain and logical thinking to the left, Flaherty notes that people who have a severed connection between the brain's hemispheres are notably lacking in creativity. At a neurological level, creativity appears to be the result of the *interaction and communication* between the hemispheres. Neither hemisphere dominates, but in the process of creative writing, there is an alternation between generating text and editing text in different areas of the brain. The emotional pressure to write comes from the limbic system deep inside the brain. This system is richly connected to the temporal lobes, which understand words and give rise to ideas. Finally, the frontal lobes organize and edit the material. Of special interest is the neurologic condition called *hypergraphia,* in which people produce voluminous quantities of writing. This symptom typically occurs in people with disorders of the brain's temporal lobes and most commonly takes place during the days and weeks between temporal lobe seizures. Dostoyevsky may be the most famous writer who suffered from this disorder.

We can make one additional detour, into a more poetic description of "the strange science of writing" proposed by Hélène Cixous. In *Three Steps on the Ladder of Writing* (1993), Cixous discusses "The School of the Dead," "The School of Dreams," and "The School of Roots." In "The School of the Dead" she proposes that something or someone must die for good writing to be born. "The School of Dreams" incorporates her view that dreams play a crucial role in literary inspiration and output, and "The School of Roots" explores the importance of depth in the "nether realms" in all aspects of writing. In a curious fashion, Cixous's ideas about deep, unconscious elements in the creative process bring us full circle to theories originally proposed by psychoanalysts, though Freud himself said, "Before the problem of the creative artist, analysis must, alas, lay down its arms."[9]

With all these theories and this research in mind, we can now read this anthology of firsthand accounts written by poets as they describe the impact of psychiatric treatment on their creative process. Gwyneth Lewis's "Dark Gifts" begins this collection with a vivid description of her ongoing struggle with severe depression and earlier history of self-treatment with alcohol. She describes how depression "strips you of everything that makes you feel like a creative, contributing member of a family or society." Treatment with psychotherapy and medication has given her the strength to maintain her creativity and become the first National Poet of Wales, even as she struggled—and continues to struggle—with recurrent episodes of illness.

J. D. Smith, in "The Desire to Think Clearly," tells of how he overcame many obstacles to treatment before finding a combination of medication and psychotherapy to help him "think clearly" and meet the challenges of chronic depression and what he defines as "self-medication" with alcohol. With effective treatment, Smith has become more playful in his work, less self-critical, and he is able to expand the themes of his poems with a greater sense of his place in the history of poetry and the human family.

In her essay, "A Crab, an Eggplant, a Tree, a Goldfish, a Cow, an Apple, a Candle: A Therapist," Denise Duhamel describes her psychotherapy treatment just after completion of her MFA. Seeking help for "chaos control," including symptoms of binge eating, binge drinking, anxiety, and depression, Duhamel's psychotherapy has freed her to break new ground in contemporary poetry with work that explores previously taboo themes, including bulimia and violence.

Thomas Krampf, who has been diagnosed in the past with schizophrenia, shares the remarkable story of jumping from a hospital window during a period of psychosis and recounts how he has spent his life "Perfecting the Art of Falling." In his poignant essay, Krampf details how an unconventional form of psychiatric treatment using orthomolecular strategies provided relief, allowed him to write poetry, and enhanced his ability to tap into "blind channels of energy . . . to get them out before I got hurt."

"My Name Is Not Alice," by Ren Powell, examines the challenges associated with the treatment of bipolar disorder. Powell confirms the tremendous outpouring of work that can occur during a manic episode, but she believes that imaginative ideas generated during a manic episode require the clear thinking and craft of stable mental functioning to be transformed into an artistic creation. Her trenchant essay also explores common myths about creativity in people with bipolar disorder.

Jesse Millner describes his chronic sense of sadness as "My Oldest Voice." Millner overcame a history of fifteen years of heavy drinking, achieved sobriety, and eventually sought treatment with antidepressant medication. As he responded to treatment, his creative work has evolved: he earned an MFA degree in poetry, pursues a career in writing, writes more effectively, and has become more fully present when he reads his work to others—but he has never quite lost the sadness "at the heart of me. My shadow, my oldest voice."

Obsessive-compulsive disorder and post-traumatic stress disorder are potentially paralyzing conditions that Vanessa Haley discusses in "How I Learned to Count to Four and Live with the Ghosts of Animals." With psychotherapeutic treatment, Haley has learned to stop her tendency to shut down and dissociate, processes that have been major obstacles to both her healing and her creativity. Poetry has become an adaptive coping strategy that helps "rebuild my lost self."

David Budbill, in "The Uses of Depression: The Way Around Is Through," guides the reader along a Buddhist path of coping with severe depression. Rather than treating depression with medication (which Budbill cannot tolerate, owing to the side effects), he practices the "give in" method of resigning himself to the "Angel of Depression." Budbill also points out the usefulness of the sense of emptiness and failure that comes with depression and how these states contribute to his creative process.

In "In the Middle of Life's Journey," Jack Coulehan describes the dramatic benefits of psychotherapy and medication in relieving his symptoms of chronic anxiety and obsessive traits. Psychotherapy has freed him to become a writer (which he believes has saved his life), and he details the significant evolution in the quality of his writing after medication treatment.

Renée Ashley, in "Basic Heart: Depression and the Ordinary," defines depression as an "ordinary" part of her daily life, part of her "basic heart." Medication, psychotherapy, and a degree of "resignation" to her chronic condition have provided partial benefit for her, but she remains terrified of the next depressive episode. Even with her terror, Ashley is still able to maintain her motivation and tenacity to keep writing.

"Food for Thought," by Caterina Eppolito, reveals the thread that connects anorexia nervosa, psychotherapeutic treatment, and creativity. Eppolito compares writing in poetic form to the symptoms of anorexia nervosa, with the intense restriction of words in poetic writing being similar to the anorexic's restriction of calories. Intensive psychotherapy has finally allowed her to transform her writing from the detachment of the third person into the first person, to acknowledge and express what she actually feels, and to find her authentic voice.

Barbara F. Lefcowitz explores the impact of her psychoanalytically oriented psychotherapy in "From Bog to Crystal." Her therapy included a focus on her unconscious creative process as well as her relationship with her therapist. Lefcowitz, who was highly attuned to her therapist's approval/disapproval, reflected on her poetry with her therapist, and she discloses a moment when the therapist made specific suggestions about a poem as part of the treatment process.

Martha Silano journeyed "In the Country of Motherhood," only to experience a severe episode of postpartum psychosis. She found a psychiatrist who provided abundant support, education, medication, and a strong therapeutic relationship, which "helped me create poetry that reaches beyond not only my own insecurities and fears. . . . I was writing poems with a more universal, all-encompassing vision."

"Down the Tracks: Bruce Springsteen Sang to Me," by Liza Porter, takes the reader on a stormy ride with a Bruce Springsteen soundtrack.

Porter has traveled the territory of depression, childhood sexual molestation, date rape, "unexpressed anger . . . drinking, drugging, destroying myself with bulimia, anorexia, compulsive exercising, dangerous men." Eventually, she finds a psychiatrist who defines her situation as one of "clinical depression," which has been treated successfully with medication. As her depression recedes, Porter notices, "My creative process, and therefore my voice, matures . . . I gain the focus and follow-through to discover the exact words and images to express what I want to say."

Andrew Hudgins suffered for years with anxiety and multiple physical symptoms, including "tics, twitches, allergies, tooth grinding, acid reflux, migraines." He tried psychotherapy, which was unsuccessful, and eventually took Paxil, which has given him a sense of "Chemical Zen." By turning down his level of anxiety, he finds, "pleasure spreads through my work in a more discernable way," and he has developed a greater sense of satisfaction with the quality of his writing.

In the closing essay, "Psychopharmacology and Its Discontents," Chase Twichell describes her severe episodes of recurrent depression, which were ineffectively controlled with medication for more than thirty years. When she was in her fifties, Twichell consulted a psychiatrist, who refined her diagnosis to bipolar II disorder, and this new diagnosis finally led to an effective medication regimen. Twichell finds herself "on an even keel," which enables her to continue her creative quest "to try to understand what it means to experience the world."

The poets whose essays you will read have created some of our finest poetry. Their stories deepen our understanding of how people overcome tremendous suffering and adversity, how we can be resilient in the face of severe trauma, and how, with effective treatment and tremendous motivation, poets can maintain their creativity. I am deeply appreciative of all the poets who have had the courage to reveal their private experiences to help us understand the creative process.

NOTES

1. Paul L. Mariani, *William Carlos Williams: A New World Naked* (New York: W. W. Norton, 1990), 665.

2. Glen Gabbard and Krin Gabbard, *Psychiatry and the Cinema* (Washington, DC: American Psychiatric Association Press, 1999).

3. Carl Elliott and Todd Chambers, *Prozac as a Way of Life* (Chapel Hill: University of North Carolina Press, 2004).

4. Alice Flaherty, *The Midnight Disease: The Drive to Write, Writer's Block, and the Creative Brain* (Boston: Houghton Mifflin Co., 2004), 66.

5. Albert Rothenberg, *Creativity and Madness: New Findings and Old Stereotypes* (Baltimore: Johns Hopkins University Press, 1990), 8.

6. Ibid., 9.

7. Ibid., 41.

8. Ibid., 13.

9. James Strachey et al., eds., *The Standard Edition of the Complete Psychological Works of Sigmund Freud,* "Dostoevsky and Parricide" (London: Hogarth Press, 1928), 21: 177.

One

DARK GIFTS

GWYNETH LEWIS, DPhil

FOR THE FORTUNATELY UNINITIATED, it's difficult to comprehend how depression strips you of everything that makes you feel like a creative, contributing member of a family or society. After a severe episode of depression, which kept me home from work for most of a year, colleagues repeatedly asked me, "Were you writing?" For a good deal of my sick leave, I'd been unable to lift a pen, get out of bed, or speak for more than a minute or two. I lived without energy, sense of humor, charm, or any of the imaginative spark that makes the future look like a desirable place to inhabit. I became Woman in a Dressing Gown. At my worst, the duvet on my bed looked like a body bag and I was the corpse inside it.

So, no, I wasn't writing, but I was making mental notes. People who don't have depression are fond of commenting that many of its victims are gifted creatively, as if this made up for the sporadic visits to one's emotional underworld. When I'm well, writing is at the very center of my life and is a powerful force for health. To write, though, I have to be feeling happy, to have a surplus of vitality that allows me to be more alive and quicker than usual, see colors more vividly, hear rhythms more subtly, and have access to all my bodily sensations. In fact, I have to be in a state of hyperawareness that is the direct opposite of the half-life of depression.

Dylan Thomas described the condition of being a poet as walking over broken glass on your eyeballs. Since I was a child, I've lacked an emotional epidermis. This is good for writing—it means I can sense a lot—but bad for one's daily equilibrium. When I was young, my mother would try to "toughen" me up by mocking many of my childish raptures. This had the effect of making me ashamed of my most extreme esthetic reactions. Many years later, when I was a student at

Columbia University's Graduate Writing Division, I nearly cried with relief to hear Nobel Laureate Joseph Brodsky warn a class of poets to "beware of the mockers." The last thing a poet needs is to be self-conscious about his or her reactions when they're already considered, let us say, unusual by conventional society. It took me years of therapy and poetic practice to unlearn the habit of self-censorship, particularly in the early stages of composing a poem, when I need to cast my net as widely as possible, without worrying if I'm upsetting anybody else with the material I'm catching. Anything unacceptable can, legitimately, be screened out at the editing stage, but if that full emotion isn't there in the first draft, the poem is very likely to be thin and uninteresting. It will have no subcutaneous fat.

I started writing poetry when I was seven. One rainy Easter holiday, I was bored, stuck inside the house. Suddenly, I started to compose a long rhyming narrative poem about the rain. This activity made me happier than anything I knew. The project of shaping the real world into a pattern that sounded beautiful thrilled me deeply and compensated, in a way, for the washout of a holiday. I showed this epic to my mother, who made corrections to the spelling. She was an English teacher, and this pattern continued for many years, until I learned not to show her my writing. Depression is shot like a dark thread through our family history. My grandmother took to her bed at a young age and used emotional manipulation to keep the rest of the family in line. I grew up observing my mother's crippling episodes, when she would take to her bed for days at a time and the rest of us had to creep around the house, careful not to set off her rage and despair.

Having learned how destructive depression can be, I was horrified to undergo a first episode in my early twenties. By then I had stopped writing altogether and was reading English at Cambridge University, a course of study guaranteed to make one feel creatively inadequate alongside Wordsworth, Keats, and other literary giants. I fell in with a sociable, rackety crowd and stopped studying. I now know that, for me, not writing is as unsafe as driving a car in the dark without headlights: I need to write to be fully conscious of my own life. I suffered a breakdown that led me to repeat my second year of studies, during which I began to realize that if I was to be well in the long term, I needed to rediscover the project of poetry on my own terms. I remember walking down Sidney Sussex Street and knowing that I desperately wanted to understand poetry and that to do so I would need to change my life. So began the long discipline of reading and internal discovery in which I am still engaged today.

After my final exams in Cambridge, I fled on a scholarship to the United States, where I was lucky enough to study with Seamus Heaney, Joseph Brodsky, and Derek Walcott, among other poets. They helped me begin to pick out a way of truth telling in words that would allow me to sidestep my own dishonesties. I consider myself fortunate to have a craft and an artistic tradition that show me how best to embark on such difficult discoveries and allow me to travel in the company of other poets. While we use language, we are never speaking alone.

Poets are constantly translating between nonverbal states of mind and language, but they do this by using poetic meter, which allows them to speak with a sound that, because of its previous use by other poets in a tradition, is larger than their individual voice. Meter, as Joseph Brodsky defined it, is reorganized time, which makes sense of W. H. Auden's statement that "time worships language." But rhyme adds another dimension to the mechanism. Poets don't compose poems starting at the first word and ending with the last (even though this might be the order in which they write them down). When you have reached a certain level of facility, rhymes come faster than grammatical sense, so you often compose your lines backward from the rhyme word. This process gives the poet a fast track to his or her unconscious, allowing surprising and mysterious conjunctions of sound and sense to surface.

Such utterance out of a collective sound gives the poet some kind of proof against the onslaughts of unconscious material that, if faced in a less corporately developed language, might be too much to endure. I was fascinated to hear the late Ted Hughes say that one of his regrets in life was that he had written so much prose. He seemed to imply that, if he'd kept to poetry, he might not have succumbed to the cancer that killed him, as if poetic meter were a lead apron he should have worn when dealing with his radioactive personal life.

By the time I returned to the United Kingdom, to do my doctorate at Oxford, I had established writing poetry as my priority in life but was far from being out of depression's woods. Over the years I had discovered alcohol as a way of self-medicating for low spirits. It stopped me from feeling painful emotions, helped me to sleep, and, in company, gave me false confidence. It was also the drug of choice in the bohemian circles of poets and journalists in which I now turned. For a while I labored under the delusion that being drunk helped me write. After all, hadn't Dylan Thomas achieved good results by translating alcoholic raptures onto the page? I used to keep notes of my altered states of mind under the influence of drink in the hope that they would offer startling new images for poems. They didn't. It was impossible to decipher my handwriting, and I kept throwing up. Another poetic myth bites the dust.

Alcohol is a powerful depressant, and its abuse propelled me into a new spiral of despair. Through my doctor I was referred to the Warneford Hospital for group therapy, which I hated. When I moved back to my home city to live, I was sent to see a psychiatrist who also practiced as a psychotherapist. I couldn't believe my luck when I discovered that this doctor also read poetry and so understood many of my artistic crises. It seems to me miraculous that I was able to have nearly fifteen years of weekly therapy free on the National Health Service, and I took full advantage of it. I'm sure that the chance to have such a high-quality conversation helped, literally, to keep me alive.

When I eventually realized that I had become hooked on alcohol and that my only chance of writing anything was to stop drinking, I was able to use a poem to explore the catastrophic effect of such drugs on creativity. A friend told me that he used to hide a half bottle of vodka in a hedge he knew, so that he could drink from it on the way to work. In "The Hedge" I imagined becoming stuck in a beech border:

> . . . you'd scarcely believe
> the strength in a hedge that has set its mind
> on holding a person in its vice of leaves
>
> and this one was proving a real bind.
> With a massive effort, I took the full strain
> and tore up the hedgerow, which I flicked up behind
>
> me, heavy and formal as a wedding train.

The poem tells the fate of a woman who tries to hide her anomalous hair-do but who, as she dies, submits to her addiction as a "narrowness, a slowly closing eye." Without this poem I would never have learned that my own difficulties, of which I'd been ashamed, could be the basis of wildly flamboyant poetry exploring the nature of psychological pain. At readings, more than ten years later, I'm still regularly asked for "The Hedge."

Things went well for me creatively in the nineties. I published six books, three in Welsh and three in English, and was awarded prizes. Having decided that I would rather be employed full time than endure the hand-to-mouth existence of the jobbing poet, I worked in the BBC as a television producer. In the morning I would write before putting on a suit and makeup. Weekends I spent away reading in festivals all over the country and, sometimes, abroad. Leighton, my husband, tried to warn me that I was doing too much, but I was so pleased to be living productively that I thought nothing of running two careers simultaneously.

During this time, I had been working hard in therapy trying to understand why I suffered from a low-grade chronic depression. With my psychotherapist I explored the history of my writing and how that had been co-opted and then rejected by important people in my life who had wanted to control me. I learned how those who are too afraid to put themselves on the line creatively resent a loved one's doing so and can attack poetry as a rival. This was never overt, but the outcome had been devastating for me. Subconsciously I'd equated the part of me that wanted to write with the betrayer of my most intimate relations. Later, I explored this dilemma in a poetic fairy tale, in which a daughter was destroyed by the conflict between two parental figures:

A FANCIFUL MARRIAGE

A blank, she became the board for their games:
The words on her face were never the same
as they played hard scrabble with desperate hands

. . . .

sure that her mirror could save their souls.
Till her own went missing. Then, how she ran
chasing its radiant flickering

down alleys of phantasmagoria

. . . .

glinting through chasms, past chimeras
that flayed her of feeling and left her for dead.

You can't manipulate a poet who's fully committed to writing because he or she is listening to a subtle but compelling rhythm that is linked to his or her most authentic self. This is why totalitarian states can't abide poets and sometimes kill those who refuse to serve the state's ideology.

In the face of apparent success, the last thing I expected was to experience an even more debilitating episode of depression. One morning I was driving to work when I began to cry. I went home, put myself to bed, and slept almost continuously for two weeks. It was five months until I began to feel even remotely like myself again and a year before I could return to work. Within hours I knew that my blood chemistry was seriously disordered because of a neurological nausea, a dry retching through all my nerves, which I knew I wouldn't be able to stand without help. I remember screaming at Leighton that, this time, I needed drugs. The next morning we went to my doctor, who prescribed Seroxat (paroxetine). The medication was a blessing in that it opened up a vital space between me and the emotional horrors that were squeezing the breath out of me. My psychiatrist suggested that I keep a mood chart, and because of this, I was able to see when Seroxat stopped working. I changed to venlafaxine (Effexor), which suited me, and I stayed on it for a couple of years.

Because I'd been seeing a psychiatrist weekly for nearly ten years, there was no doubt about the diagnosis of unipolar depression. We had spoken about the possibility of my being bipolar in the past but had used the checklist of symptoms in the *Diagnostic and Statistical Manual*, 4th edition, to confirm that I am unipolar. We checked this because I do have an unusual amount of energy for long periods and am able to work more productively than many people. This, however, is never without cost, and I pay for prolonged periods of work with equivalent barren periods, during which I have to rest and recover. Over the years I've learned to notice that hyperactivity is a reliable indicator of when I'm about to go down. It's as if my body knows that it won't be able to sustain its current workload for much longer and that if some project needs to be completed, it had better be done quickly. My goal now is to learn how to work more consistently, so that I avoid extremes of workaholism and lassitude, but this self-control is an ongoing struggle. In my case, the fatigue indicator that tells most people that they need to recharge their batteries is broken, so I need another form of discipline to stop me from driving myself into the ground. When I fail at this, my husband resorts to shouting at me, and that usually, though not always, works.

By the time I'd recovered from that episode of depression, I finally understood that writing and working full time was no longer a sustainable combination for me. I took voluntary redundancy from my job and, with the payment, bought a sailing yacht. Leighton and I had always wanted to undertake a long voyage, so we set off to circumnavigate the globe. Neither of us had sailed before, though Leighton had been in the merchant marine, and leaving the United Kingdom for European waters put us through a steep learning curve. Whereas I had been glad to take venlafaxine while I was coming out of my depression, it was only when we were at sea that we noticed the drawbacks of the drug. It seemed to dull the speed of my reactions and make me indifferent to problems. This is useful if you're feeling hysterical but is not a good thing if you're being blown toward a rock and need to think what to do with the sails to avoid the danger of shipwreck. I resolved, with my psychiatrist's agreement, to come off the medication slowly, and I did.

I was not to know that life was about to become ten times harder. Our marriage, which had been extremely happy, seemed to be unravelling under the pressures of a new environment. After a very challenging fifteen months making our way from Cardiff, Wales, to Gibralter, to Ceuta, Spanish Morocco, on the coast of North Africa, we discovered that Leighton was suffering from Stage IV non-Hodgkin lymphoma. Under the stress of feeling so ill, Leighton had turned into a negative, angry man, very different from the person I'd married. It seemed to me that we might well be heading toward divorce. We left the boat in Ceuta, a Spanish enclave in Morocco, and returned to Wales so that he could undergo chemotherapy. I looked after him through this ordeal and was astonished to find that, although I was under substantial stress, I wasn't depressed. Going into winter, with nowhere to live (we'd rented out our house) and uncertain whether Leighton was going to live or die, I still felt alive and could see dark gifts in each day.

During the seven months of Leighton's chemo cycle, I sat at home with him and wrote *Two in a Boat,* my account of our voyage, using it as a lamp to guide us through what had become very confused emotional waters. For me, the way out of the crisis was directly through that book, and I was aware of trying to sort out for both of us whether or not we should stay together. I showed him each chapter as I finished it. He was subdued to begin with, but then he acknowledged that, painful though it was, what I had written was true. I think that book saved our marriage.

Only two of my eight books have been written while taking antidepressants, so I find it very difficult to distinguish between the effect of the medication and a development in my own style away from ornamentation and toward greater simplicity (which, of all literary effects, requires the most skill and is the most difficult to achieve). Even if it was proven that antidepressants adversely affected my ability as a poet, I'd still take them. After being a zombie for months, being able to write at all is a miracle, and that participation in the creative discipline, rather than a more objective measure of excellence, is the bottom line for me.

Sunbathing in the Rain: A Cheerful Book on Depression was my first book of nonfiction, and I wrote it extremely quickly after my most serious episode, before I could forget how it felt. It was an attempt to produce the kind of book a depressive could read while in the middle of a low, so it was written in short paragraphs, for those with zero concentration. Because I made use of painful experiences in the book, the distancing effect of the medication while I wrote it was an asset—like wearing an oven glove when checking on a red-hot casserole. I was aware of tempting fate by offering advice to those undergoing depression, knowing full well that following such counsel would be very difficult for me during my next bout. Fortunately, I never deluded myself that I had been cured, and a recent, much milder episode, reminded me of the ongoing adjustments I need to make in order to continue to be able to write. There is a very close connection between depression and creativity, but it's not of the crudely compensatory kind usually described by casual observers.

If you're a poet, writing isn't an optional extra in your life; it's a fundamental part of your creative economy. For me, poetry represents the minimum amount of reality that I require in order to live well. Any lies in my thinking, any self-indulgence simply won't scan, and I have to abandon those ideas of victimhood and move on to thoughts that will work practically, both in the poem and in my life. Without poetry as a guarantor of straight thinking, what I'm living isn't my genuine life but a forgery. It may look plausible, but it wasn't meant for me.

Poetry has acquired a fluffy image that is totally at odds with its real nature. It's not pastel colors, but blood red and black. If you don't obey it as a force in your life, it will tear you to pieces. The Furies are the creative processes' revenge if you refuse to embody them. This rejection is more than creative sabotage, it's impiety. The gods always avenge it. Meter and rhyme help to earth that force and find a safe way of incorporating it in words. This is because poetry is a form of energy that links the electricity of your truth to the world around you. Abusing this process, which links deeply into the subconscious, is likely to cause an artist big psychological problems. Unwritten poems are to be feared. Some of this terror is conveyed by a dream notebook I once kept during a period of not writing:

Have been racked by dreams of guilt and violence. Last night poetry was out to get me. I had to foresee the blows and avoid them.

1. Through a pane of glass, to which I had my back, coming through with a pick-axe which melted the pane and my skull like ice . . .

2. Standing at a bus stop, it comes at me with a curved axe, with a sweeping movement from behind, using the haft's weight to make the blow accurate.

It's hardly surprising that I now dread disobeying my own creative gods more than I hate displeasing other people. However, it has taken me years of therapy and artistic discipline to recognize when I'm doing the one thing or the other and be able to choose between them.

One of the most important things I learned in therapy was that I had, in key relationships in the past, confused other people's thoughts and emotions with my own. Because of my own lack of confidence, I'm often drawn to strong personalities who have definite views. Agreeing with them takes away the often painful struggle toward discovering what I myself think about an event or an issue. Over the years I've learned to use poetry as a white stick to guide me through terrain that I find difficult to discern. Time and time again in therapy, I'd be astonished to discover that my own view of a situation wasn't at all the same as the one I'd absorbed from someone close to me. In fact, I'd find that I had very strong opinions of my own. My writing poetry—which freed me to see things in my own way—was a threat to anybody who wanted to manipulate me, and it attracted their hostility. Now I tend to see such attacks as a sign that I'm doing something right, not the opposite, but I've never been happy to participate in workshops because they leave me feeling unreasonably vulnerable.

I've often been puzzled by the higher than average incidence of depression and suicide among, particularly, poets. It seems to suggest that we're delicate creatures, unable to stand up to the rigors of real life. If you think about it, though, poets spend time in the kind of territory most people will take a good deal of trouble to avoid. They work alone, in an occupation that is unrewarded materially and socially. The discipline of meter and rhyme is demanding and constantly humiliating to the practitioner. It takes years to even begin to be able to master the craft of poetry, let alone use it to express the most difficult emotions.

You start a poem, and the first draft is terrible. Next day, you get the first two lines into shape, but the rest is even worse; you have to leave it then because, on that day, your unconscious can't tell you any more. Third day and you're half way through and oh, the anxiety, the fear of not pulling it off. Fourth day, will you get the end? Poems require this daily input of incomplete knowledge, as if you were sewing time into the fabric of your work. The poetic mind has an unusual tolerance for living in this painful gap between the ideal and the botched reproduction. Far from being wimps, poets simply spend more time than the rest of the population in this hazardous landscape.

At certain stages of the creative cycle, depression is, quite simply, the enemy of artistic production. But the big breakthrough in my attitude toward it came when I began to realize that, for me, depression is not a condition separate from that creative cycle but is part of it—albeit a dark, difficult, and demanding part. Indeed, over the years I've learned that depression is one of the most reliable guardians of my life as a poet. It's like the fuse in a house with suspect wiring: it's the weakest part of the system, which ensures the safety of the whole. It pulls the plug when I'm in danger of burning the house down by doing too much. It leaves me in the dark, but at least I'm alive. Its appearance is always unwelcome but, once I've come to grips with what it's telling me about how I've been squandering my inner resources, I'm never worse off than I was before its visitation. Indeed, I have come to value its dark gifts sufficiently that I can imagine it as a visiting angel—not a soft-focus sentimental celestial being, but one that is more deeply in touch with reality than I am:

ANGEL OF DEPRESSION

Why would an angel choose to come here
if it weren't important? . . .

. . . .
Don't say it's an honour to have fought
with depression's angel. It always wears
the face of my loved ones as it tears
the breath from my solar plexus, grinds
my face in the ever-resilient dirt.
Oh yes, I'm broken but my limp
is the best part of me. And the way I hurt.

GWYNETH LEWIS

Two

THE DESIRE TO THINK CLEARLY

J. D. SMITH, MA

FOR A POET, SEEKING TREATMENT for depression is to break with an implicit social contract. To the extent that the culture at large has a view of poets, beyond acknowledging their existence as a strange but seldom seen life form, such as a platypus or giant squid, that view is based on the Romantic myth of the poet as a strange, distraught creature, preferably consumptive, who occasionally breaks forth in song or a dirge. The poet in this view is morose so that others do not have to be, a pack mule for the collective burden of consciousness.

I had not been consulted on this arrangement, though, and even before I wrote anything worthwhile I wanted out, because depression did far more to obstruct than encourage my writing. Coming of age in the 1970s and 1980s, in the shadow of the confessional poets and during a time of growing narcissism in American culture, I was nearly predestined to plumb the depths of my angst in verse, but the results amounted to more or less elaborate ways of saying "I feel miserable and hopeless," though with line breaks. In one of the perverse defeats of youth, I had to admit that Plath, Sexton, and Lowell had "better" material to work with and more profound psychiatric problems.

Besides, whatever gifts I possess as a poet lend themselves more to engagement with the outside world than portraying inner states. Being a poet *in* despair does not necessarily make one a poet *of* despair. My own inner states have existed largely as an obstacle to concentrating on other, more interesting issues. The depression that had mercifully turned me away from gregarious and time-consuming professions such as selling real estate or running for office, which might have distracted me from poetry altogether, had also kept me from paying sufficient attention to subjects beyond myself.

More than a decade after the fact, I can still remember my exact words when the doctor asked me what I was expecting from the medication (fluoxetine hydrochloride, aka Prozac) that would finally work for me.

"I want to think clearly."

If nothing else, it would have been a novelty. By then I had spent most of my life seeing the world through whatever is the opposite of rose-colored glasses. Still, some part of my psyche stood apart from the larger tumult and realized that things felt far worse than they should.

What I said to the doctor next does not stay with me verbatim, perhaps because it wasn't completely honest. I stated, more or less, "I'm not looking for a happy pill."

I should have added, "anymore." It wasn't for lack of trying. By the time raves and Ecstasy had entered the culture I was too old to travel in those circles without feeling like a creepy hanger-on. Before then I had used alcohol in repeated attempts to feel right or, in the jargon I later learned, self-medicate. Luck, or grace, or an incongruous sense of self-preservation based on seeing *The Lost Weekend* at an impressionable age kept me from following some of my relatives—perhaps self-medicating as well—into alcoholism.

Thinking clearly seemed to be all I could hope for. Thinking clearly, though, might let me write without the sabotage of self-doubt, trouble concentrating, and difficulty in sustaining projects or working through multiple drafts—followed by guilt and self-loathing for my failures.

I had somehow managed to endure talking therapies and previous attempts at medication without taking a razorblade to my wrists. I had even managed to write passably at times, though my "successes" were short poems that needed little revision and that were largely confined to my own concerns. The following poem, "Shortness," which I wrote as an undergraduate, embodies all of these tendencies.

You are king nowhere,
not even in your skin's space
that one large hand can
drag away or crack.
Your coins are thin, picked up off the ground,
and no one will take them
when you reach the bar, debate your age,
strut length into toy legs.
You look close, seeing things
parallel to flight below radar range
the way maple seeds fall,

the flutist's tapping foot,
how a lie hides in the extra half inch
you tell your blind dates.
You keep a second soul on hand
in case the first grows large and breaks.

I still like the poem, though less than I used to, but it was not the only kind of poem I wanted to write in a world of political strife and ecological danger, and in a national poetry already too much given to solipsism.

Even when I could write, it was usually in the middle of the night. Like many depressives, I started my days in torpor and was not fully alert until the rest of the world was ready to go to bed. This put me at odds with class schedules and later work schedules, as I dragged myself through the daylight hours before and after the late hours in which I found a certain amount of tranquility and ability to work.

This pattern outlasted years of seeking help in fits and starts according to the vagaries of insurance coverage, out-of-pocket ability to pay, and my own sense of futility. As an undergraduate in the early 1980s, ages ago in terms of attitudes toward depression, I was subjected to routine blood work and questions about whether I experienced hallucinations or heard voices and was told that I could not be both depressed and anxious at the same time, regardless of how I felt. Medication was not indicated, and the counseling that followed mainly allowed me to discuss how I saw my circumstances in the darkest possible light. During my first of three bouts of graduate school—another sign of clouded thinking—I was given an intake appointment with one of the last hardline Freudians in captivity. The clinical hour was filled with his psychosexual questions and my attempts to evade them as premature prying. There was no second appointment.

Round two of graduate school, this time in creative writing, found me seeking counseling again at a time when my remaining enfant terrible tendencies collided with professors who wrote with greater skill than they taught; it was also at this time that my great-grandfather died. Several sessions with a psychologist who was not brandishing an agenda proved a relief in itself, but nothing that allowed me to move beyond writing as a passive transcription of inspiration when the impulse broke through my self-doubt.

The last semester of that program afforded me my first experience with medication, a clinical trial of nefazodone, later marketed as Serzone. Though my moods improved quickly, and I learned the pleasure of being a "good responder," putting together my thesis largely distracted me from writing new poems. This distraction, combined with the brevity of the trial, prevented me from seeing what I might have done with a longer respite from dark thoughts. The clinical trial ended shortly before I received my degree and moved several states away to my parents' home, where I had neither immediate job prospects nor insurance. As depression carried a greater stigma then, it was several years before I could discuss my condition openly with my parents or others, so I could hardly ask for money that would go to no apparent purpose— even if I had known of a commercially available drug that would work.

For another four years, from 1989 to 1993, I tried without success to recapture that relatively placid state. Variously underemployed as an adjunct instructor, a legislative intern, and an office temp, I scraped together money for out-of-pocket appointments with my family's general practitioner. He prescribed imipramine, a well-studied tricyclic that offered me few side effects and possibly fewer benefits for my mood, since there was no discernible improvement. We detoured once into imipramine's tricyclic cousin amitryptyline. After about ten days of feeling drugged in the wrong way, as if I were moving and breathing underwater, and writing nothing, we returned to the de facto placebo of imipramine.

Only in my third graduate program, this time in international relations—a last-ditch effort to be "practical"—did I find the right combination of physician and pharmaceuticals, beginning with the appointment I mentioned above. While finishing my coursework and writing my thesis on security in the Balkans I found myself writing more poems and starting to think about writing in other genres. Since graduating from that program in 1995 I have maintained a fairly steady schedule of consultation and medication. It is also since then that I have published my first two collections of poems, as well as numerous essays and stories.

My course of treatment is almost embarrassingly nondescript, and it will make neither medical nor literary history. Every two months I have an appointment during which my psychiatrist largely gives me the opportunity to think aloud about the state and direction of my life for the duration of the therapeutic hour. Sometimes I talk myself into realizing that things are not going as well as I indicated at the beginning of the appointment, and at other times talking, like writing, gives me a way to think through a problem and discover, or rediscover, my underlying concerns. We usually end each appointment by scheduling the next one and checking on whether my prescription for generic fluoxetine hydrochloride—usually the twenty-milligram dose that I had first tried—will last until our next meeting.

The kind of before-and-after pictures that advertise weight loss plans and hair replacement treatments are not available, and I cannot offer a dramatic testimonial for a product or service that everyone must try now. I can only say what has worked for me over time.

Outlines of the effects of treatment are starting to emerge. With many of my personal dilemmas now resolved or at least contained, I find my sensibility drawn to subjects and objects well beyond myself. The materials of the self—vocabulary, temperament, life experience— inevitably provide the lenses through which the materials of art are perceived and conveyed, but focusing those lenses on topics other than myself is a growing source of pleasure for me. I have written poems that were cries of the heart or notes for a counseling session, but sometimes a poem such as "Pistachios," quoted in part below, which primarily expresses a mind at play:

> Clams of dry land,
> suspended mid-gape,
> they are, as well, truncated
> busts of hatchlings that peep
> for an imminent feeding,
> and parentheses, poised
> to shelter a digression.

In writing that poem I did not feel the need to "swing for the fences," to fall back on sports imagery, or to address a major issue; I simply felt the need to follow sound and metaphor. This poem is clearly not Milton's sonnet on his blindness, and it does not pretend to be, but I suspect that I and others would be ever so slightly poorer without it.

More than to play in language, though, I am drawn to social and moral concerns, such as the relationship between the individual and history and the ruptured relationship between the human and natural worlds. I have always been interested in issues of the larger world as an escape from my own concerns, but now I find them simply more interesting.

Thinking relatively clearly has increasingly allowed me to engage with the discipline of formal verse. While formal poems can sometimes seemingly come from nowhere, especially in the case of epigrams and short light verse, any formal poem longer than a handful of lines usually requires me to sketch out phrases to find an appropriate meter and consider meaningful line breaks, or to list rhyming words until I find possibilities that seem remotely natural. The inability to concentrate and a tendency to give up difficult projects in despair and self-loathing had previously prevented me from following through on formal poems on any consistent basis. Acknowledging that difficulty is inherent in formal verse and not just the result of my own limitations, and embracing that difficulty as a useful challenge has led me to poems and insights within poems that I would otherwise have set aside or never attempted.

My "healthy" state—to whatever extent we approach the Promised Land of Mental Health—additionally allows me to look at drafts of my darker poems to see whether it is merely the depression talking or whether the tone matches the content of the poem and bears some relation to the facts of the world at large. This can lead to extensive revision or to the wholesale abandonment of poems that fail to carry their own lugubrious weight, which has saved me the embarrassment of reading on stage or publishing poems too self-pitying or poorly turned to inflict on anyone.

Thinking more and more clearly over time, I have, as social workers would say, tried to objectify my experiences, including depression, and more nearly master them through exploration and even an occasional moment of self-parody:

DEPRESSIVE

Overshadowed by a blade of grass,
soaked by one rain-drop,
struck down by a dandelion seed.

Carried off by a sparrow
that will soon despair
of the bitter taste in the flesh,
the millstone's weight.

As I once explored the questions of youth, I am beginning to explore the questions of middle age, and the "I" of my earlier poems, which insisted on its uniqueness, increasingly gives way to "we," who all suffer from one malady or another and are in the same leaky boat together. In my late twenties I was fortunate enough to come across a biography of John Dryden whose author noted that "we" appears in Dryden's work more than any other pronoun. This seemed exotic at first, then an unexploited niche and a challenge to rise to, and it has allowed me to more nearly meet that challenge, as in the final stanzas of the poem "For Bad Wine":

> As, even in mid-life, we're intimidated
> by the corkscrew, the very cork,
> the intricate and solemn techniques
> and auguries of its removal,
> we look among the simple screw tops,
> such as we turned to open soda and juice
> before our first high school drink.
>
> Because we may as well toast our younger selves
> who didn't know Boone's Farm from Bordeaux,
> who knew we would get rich while doing good,
> but in the meantime had to scrimp,
> we will take the cheapest brand.
>
> Because we now know better,
> but have to save for retirement,
> we will take the large and cost-effective jug.
>
> Because we have our reasons
> and don't want to tell them again,
> we'll refill our glasses
> and drain every drop.

Yet subject matter alone does not explain the entirety of what happened as the chemistry of brain, of my being, has been changed, as the torpor in my limbs and in my head are held at bay, diminished if never lifted away altogether.

Beyond changes in subject matter, and changes in tone and form, the way I approach the act of writing, the process of composition, has changed immensely.

Uncertain of what—if anything—I was good for, at various times I have used the writing of poems as a means of attempting to justify my existence—as if anything could justify or invalidate that existence. This misunderstanding of the nature of poetry, my own or anyone else's, led me to overproduce, with self-imposed and shifting assignments of so many pages a week or poems a month, and guilt for missing the mark. If I wasn't engaged in some other form of self-loathing at the time, I could despise myself for turning into the caricature of writer as parasite, he who must always be scouring the world for "material" because he has no sensibility, interests, or inner life of his own to address. The resulting poems kept me from falling into bad company or spending too much money, but they came from a false place. Some served as exercises in form or voice, but exercises reach a point of diminishing returns; work on the barre alone never made a ballerina. Such an approach, which largely involved misguided efforts trying to make a poem out of something better suited for a story or essay, at least kept me in the habit of writing.

Except when it didn't. Which was often. The problem with attempting to justify one's existence through poetry is that the stakes of any poem become abnormally high. Writing a bad poem can provide one more reason to feel unfit to face the world, like the biblical leper who must ring a bell and cry "unclean" to warn others in his path.

One sure escape from writing bad poems is to write nothing at all, to yield to the dreaded voice of the "inner critic." This is the voice that A. E. Housman appeared to have in mind when he addressed his alter ego with the words "Terence, this is stupid stuff!"—a voice that frequently echoed in my own lower-middle-class mind when I considered how writing poems was doing nothing to help me make a living.

Instead of experiencing an appropriate fear and trembling at the prospect of disturbing the purity of a blank page, I was simply paralyzed. Who was I to attempt to say something when so many others had already done so, and were doing so even now? What made me so special? (Strangely, I seldom asked what made *others* so special.)

The changes that have allowed me to engage with the world and spend less time loathing myself apart from it, gaining what Freud called the ability to work and to love, have given me license to engage with poems in a way I might not have considered before. I can write a poem that makes me say "this sucks" yet understand that no general statement follows about my other poems or my existence in general.

If I write badly, as in previous drafts of this essay, I know it is only one bad day at the office. A bad poem is nothing but itself, harmless if tucked away, and it can be gotten out of the way en route to writing better poems. This has given me the courage to attempt new forms and topics in the knowledge that a desk drawer is a fine and private place, and a very forgiving one. My ability to contextualize bad work, to recover from it no less than any other setback, has made me more patient. A poem may start out as something hobbled, a felicitous line or two surrounded by five options for every verb, notations in parentheses about tonal lapses and over-long sentences. I can give myself permission, though, as counselors and self-help books say, to write an utter mess and improve it later, holding at bay the inner editor until there is something to improve. My identity is not tied up with immediate perfection. And revising in the long term is less intimidating; I don't have to constantly crank out finished products, or *product,* in the generic term of retail, to feel worthy of breathing someone else's air. By giving up on a goal of such industrial production, I am allowed to realize other gains. "Aurora's Lockers," a poem on the disconnect between my background and my aspirations, but a poem that seems to have value for others as well as myself, led me to engage in revision by fits and starts over twenty years—more than half my life at that point. Only then did I find a conclusion expressing both the combination of resignation and affirmation that I had been seeking:

> My laps run around Aurora.
> Back or forth is the farthest I swim away.
> Showered, I stand and work a combination,
> down to my name and wet footprints,
> facing an enclosure I've always known.

This poem was eventually published and came to anchor a segment of my second collection.

A poet constantly intent on proclaiming, a Whitman or a Mayakovsky, has little need of such patience, but a poet shaped for listening, as I apparently am, has no choice. The poem will be there, in electronic files and hard copy, and a poem that at first seemed trivial or flat, or merely a set of notes, can be sharpened over time.

The stakes have changed. There is little to lose, but much to gain. Possibly not in recognition, and certainly not in money, but in the self-realization of writing poems rather than not writing poems. Some work, some don't, but I am increasingly willing to get through the poem to see how it turns out. The end of a long, messy poem I wrote at the expense of a night's sleep (I still prefer to write at night), and one that took a great deal of revision, led me by surprise to such a realization, which I cannot paraphrase but only quote:

> It is always time to wake up.
> It is always time to dream.

Three

A CRAB, AN EGGPLANT, A TREE,

A GOLDFISH, A COW, AN APPLE, A CANDLE

A THERAPIST

DENISE DUHAMEL, MFA

IN 1988, I STARTED to see Rodney for anxiety, depression, and something we called "chaos control." I had recently received my MFA degree from Sarah Lawrence, though we rarely talked about poetry the three years I saw him. I never shared any of my poems with him, though I did dedicate my book *Girl Soldier* to his memory. Instead of poetry, Rodney and I mostly talked about my binge eating. Other topics included my binge drinking, my family history, my attraction to all the wrong men and several wrong women friends, and occasionally my frustrations with the poetry world.

When I didn't get a grant I thought I deserved, Rodney wisely said, "Give yourself your own grant." I had just received a small inheritance from my favorite uncle and Rodney suggested that I use that money to take a summer off and just write. Although I couldn't do it, although I resisted, I remember Rodney saying over and over, "Why are you waiting for outside approval?" He goaded me into owning that I was a poet no matter what, if I ever had a poem published or not. More importantly, when he asked, "Why are you waiting for outside approval?" I realized that question went to the very core of the poems themselves and what I chose to write about. Why was I waiting for approval to explore eating disorders or violence or other subjects that I worked through with Rodney but that were, I thought, taboo in the world of poetry at the time? What fairy godmother was going to come from afar with her wand in hand? In Cinderella stories from around the world, the fairy godmother can arrive in the shape of a crab, an eggplant, a tree, a goldfish, a cow, or an apple. Mine came in the form of an Australian therapist named Rodney, who had his practice in New York City.

Because of Rodney, I slowly grew less fearful about writing poems that scared me. When I timidly told him my horrible secrets, he didn't blink or gasp; sometimes he didn't even write them down on his yellow pad. I guessed that he also had problems with food, because over the years I met with him, his weight fluctuated from chubby to not so chubby to chubby again. He was always drinking Cann's diet chocolate soda, which, to me, was a giveaway that he craved sweets, too.

When I wrote a poem called "Bulimia," I wasn't even sure what to do with it. The poem was just another one of my secrets for a while. I knew it was important—important that I wrote it, that is. I didn't dare to think whether it was good or not, or whether it was a real poem. Rodney, who knew little of the poetry world, said that I should do with "Bulimia" what I'd do with any other poem. I sent "Bulimia" to about fifteen magazines over the course of five years. Most of the rejection slips were impersonal run-of-the-mill little slips of paper, but others were actually mean-spirited. One of the first editors I sent the poem to wrote that if I insisted on writing about such a subject, I should at least try to get my lines under control. Rodney said that letter meant I'd hit a nerve. Good fairy godmother that he was, he bitchily diagnosed the editor with having her own issues around eating disorders. (And that, in turn, convinced me that he had those issues too—and from then on, he and I were in even greater solidarity.) I didn't change the poem by tightening the lines. I didn't wait for approval. I kept writing poems as I sent this one out. And I was elated when the poem was finally published in *Poet Lore:*

BULIMIA

A kiss has nothing to do with sex,
she thinks. Not really. That engulfing, that trying to take
all of another in for nourishment, to become one with her,
        to become
part of her cells. The way she must have had everything
        she wanted
in the womb, without asking. Without words,
kisses have barely the slurp-sound of a man entering a woman
or sliding back out—neither movement with even the warning
        of a bark.
The Greek word "boulimia," ox hunger.
Petting those kisses are called, or sometimes necking.
She read this advice in a sex manual once: "Take the man's
        penis,
slowly at first, like you are licking melting ice cream

from the rim of a cone." But the gagging, the choke—
a hot gulp of tea, a small chicken bone, a wad of gum grown
    too big.
That wasn't mentioned. It's about what happens in her mouth
past her teeth, where there is no more control, like a waterfall—
or it being too late when the whole wedding cake is gone. . . .

When the poem was picked up for *Best American Poetry 1994* and
Literature Around the Globe in the same year, I was stunned. I had
finished my work with Rodney at that point, and I even thought about
calling him to tell him my good fortune. I decided against it, remembering the way he had of celebrating my successes without making
them a bigger deal than they were. I guessed that Rodney would have
been more interested in a new poem I was writing, about something
even more secret, than in a mere publishing credit. I was glad I hadn't
waited for outside approval to go on but had to admit that outside approval felt pretty good. Without Rodney, I probably wouldn't have been
able to write the poem, and without him, I definitely wouldn't have had
the courage to keep it in circulation as long as I did. Since then "Bulimia" has wound up in books about eating disorders, and copies sit in
folders in other therapists' offices.

When I first started seeing Rodney, I was in a destructive relationship he helped me look at, look through, and eventually leave. Bob was
my shadow, an alcoholic who was so ill I seemed sane and moderate by
comparison. Bob waited for liquor stores to open. He was losing his
teeth. He was mean. Here's part of a prose poem, "When I Was Still
Drinking," I wrote during the last few months of working with Rodney.

I went to the tarot card reader I said *I want Bob gone I want him to go away
move to New England with his new girlfriend with her Birkenstocks and braids
and leave me alone* Bob was still around calling to ask me questions about
tenant strikes or if the moon was going to be new or full that night because I had a special moon calendar my mother had given me for Christ-
mas I told the Gypsy *Bob calls and tells me what he wants to do to my body
I run into him on the street and he follows me into the movies* her office was
a storefront on 14th Street with prostitute beads separating the rest of her
house her kids who were watching Oprah and eating fistfuls of Cheerios
out of the box the Gypsy gave me candles and special paper to write Bob's
name on and instructions about water and dissolving burning paper in it
and sleeping with the water above my head which was difficult to do since
I slept in a loft bed and I was still drinking and was sure I'd get everything

wrong but I somehow followed her instructions and the water turned black which she said was very bad next I was supposed to try to get her some of Bob's hair and two hundred dollars which I did and which made me feel ashamed when I told my therapist but at least I didn't give the two hundred dollars to Bob who in addition to drinking had begun to develop a coke habit I felt ripped off and stupid when her spell didn't work and I still wanted Bob like I wanted vodka and eventually his rum even though it all made me sick the next day even though as I spoke to him and took my first sip I felt a dread and hatred and disgust and I'd tell my friend on the phone *he's a pig I loath him* right while he was sleeping there a lump on my couch I kept passing the Gypsy in front of the post office who wanted more money since she could see my problem was special since she could see so many enemies around me that I needed three white candles for protection her kids were filthy with crusted-over nostrils Bob was filthy I started using a different post office that's when I changed my lock and phone number that's when things began

Rodney was patient as I rambled about tarot cards, runes, psychics, and crystals—shortcuts to knowing the future. He saw them as a diversion, my hope to find an easy potion to get rid of my problems, but he never humiliated me. I had read a New Age book, persuading myself that Bob had something to do with one of my past lives. I had hoped to make Bob completely disappear without having to face him or face the demons in myself. But Rodney taught me otherwise. I began to take charge of situations.

Another poem I wrote while working with Rodney was "Whole." Rodney was one of the most sex-positive people I ever met. He pooh-poohed shame in all its ugly forms—shame resulting from body image issues, religion, societal pressures, and former abuse—without disregarding how all those factors play into our sex lives. The AIDS epidemic was still fairly new in the late 1980s, and Rodney fought hard against indignity of any kind. When he asked matter-of-factly if I ever masturbated, he told me later that even my neck turned purple. I realized that I tended to write about myself in the third person when I got scared, that as engaged as I was, I was also above myself, floating. When I heard about kids who instinctively masturbated on beach balls, not knowing what they were doing, I didn't really believe it. I had no memory of touching myself "down there," ever; it never had even occurred to me to do so. When I had sensations, watching something or reading something, I didn't know I could do anything to spur them on. I just let them fade. I hadn't expected much from my boyfriends and consequently had never had an orgasm when I started working with Rodney. Of course, because I was obsessed with poetry, I wondered what consequences this orgasm-less life had for my writing. Was my passivity in this one area holding me back? In the story, Cinderella is good and kind and gets noticed and rewarded by enduring abuse and neglect. But my fairy godmother, Rodney, assured me this wouldn't be the result in my case. I had to take my future and, in this one case, my crotch into my own hands:

WHOLE

I learned to masturbate late,
In my mid-twenties, with a self-help book
In my loft bed in the East Village.
A few blocks over at an underground club
people were having orgasms in public,
and on stage at the Pyramid,
Annie Sprinkle showed her cervix
to all who were interested. As I learned to dance
around the primal scream that was my clitoris,
around the pink cartoon blurb missing words,
I was in kindergarten gym again. Mr. Lynn
held his left open hand against my back
and his right open hand under the wing span
of my ribs. The forest green mat before me
was spooky, everything dark
beyond my small town.

I still felt I was on the outside looking in, still learning about sex and poetry and relationships, but as "everyone else went on," I was trying to go on too, willing to start from wherever I was. Rodney and I never got to that one revelation, that one "aha!" moment that made me who I am. I'm not even sure if there is that one moment in my case, or, if there is, if I'll remember it. I discovered instead to keep exploring, to keep being open to poetry and memory while living and writing. I've discovered that I don't need to know any answers when I write. Here's an excerpt from a poem I wrote in the summer of 2004, after seeing a documentary about Fargo, a sculptor with multiple personalities. I felt Rodney's spirit as I wrote it:

Fargo has so many different personalities, she can play
Monopoly

with herself—one of her selves throwing the dice and moving
    the shoe,
another of her selves moving the hat and landing on Water
    Works.
The big hotels and little square houses
talk to each other. I'm afraid of her sculpture—
a shadow that an opening door makes in the middle of the
    night.
Who comes into her room? Who is the woman in her
    photograph
sitting alone under the stairs? I've asked myself so many times
about my own dream of the quarter, the palm, and the penis.
Who does that penis belong to? Where did I meet it?
Did I also meet that penis in real waking life?

Did I meet that penis in the bar when I was little,
when my father, who took me there, wasn't watching?
The penis is not my father's. I know that much.
He was always so careful when he bathed us.
When he toweled us dry, he didn't even rub between our legs.
My sister and I just spread them and he made a fan
with the Cottoncrest and whipped it around, away from our
    skin,
and we air dried that way. I know he is the obvious suspect,
but I know the penis isn't his, and maybe the penis
belongs to no one real at all. The dream is
of a penis and a quarter in my palm. My palm is so small.
I'm still working it out, as they say, as therapists say, as my
    friends say,
as I guess I'm saying now in this poem.

In 1995, I heard from a friend, another poet, who had suggested I
see Rodney for therapy in the first place, that Rodney had been diagnosed with liver cancer. He was only in his early forties. It dawned on
me that I'd never thought about his age before—and, though I had
considered him a wise fairy-godmotherish sage, I now clearly remembered his baby face, his round cheeks, which never fluctuated like the
rest of his body. My friend and I talked about how we still heard his advice in our heads in moments of stress. I had thought of calling Rodney
so many times since we'd stopped meeting, yet I didn't want to be like
that hanger-on student, wanting yet another recommendation letter or

pep talk. But I called him as soon as my friend and I hung up, even though I had no idea what I would say. I'd since married and left New York with my husband for a short-term teaching job in Pennsylvania. My happiness and all my plans for the future seemed obscene. I couldn't tell Rodney any of them, and he didn't ask. I took a bus into New York. I called him again, this time from the pay phone on the corner of his street, and asked if I could bring him anything.

"Cashews," he said. He couldn't get out. He wasn't able to eat much else.

Rodney told me it was hard for him to get up, but that the woman caring for him would leave the door to his apartment unlocked. I'd never been in his apartment before, but it seemed to me it was full of the same earth-tone colors in his office. He was a stick figure on an overstuffed couch; even his chubby cheeks were gone. I asked him how he was doing, what hurt and where. He tried to eat a few nuts. I brought him a glass of water from his fridge. His eyes seemed huge. He told me he had a boyfriend, a Filipino, which let me tell him I'd married a Filipino man. We had a good laugh about that and an awkward laugh about how now he could fit in his "skinny jeans." Rodney said he was angry with God, because he had finally met someone he loved who loved him back. We both agreed it was completely unfair. I was thinking that perhaps I had become the therapist—Rodney on the couch, me in a chair. I wondered if there was any lesson to be learned, any positive spin I could possibly put on this situation. I remember thinking, *Denise, you are the fairy godmother now. Where is your magic?* But before I was able to say anything stupid, the phone, situated so that Rodney could reach it, rang. And this was the last lesson Rodney gave me. I believe it applies to living life as well as writing poetry:

He picked it up, listened for a few seconds, and then hung up without saying a word.

"A wrong number?" I asked.

"A telemarketer," he said. "I'm dying—hey, we're all dying—why waste even one syllable talking bullshit."

Four

PERFECTING THE ART OF FALLING

THOMAS KRAMPF

THE EUCLIDS

I was mugged by my favorite hickory cane.
It was down by the projected Gowanus Swimming Pool.
I fell to my knees with a gaping hole ripped in the red dirt
earth and torn wire fence of my imagination.
Unconsciously I put my hand to my nose but I didn't bleed.
I looked through the Spring leaves at a bemedaled factory chute
heavily armed and attacking ferociously across a roof.
I noticed drifting accomplished beneath the distant blue sky
the white project buildings suspiciously surrendering their eyes.
Somewhere I heard bulldozers crashing blindly through apple
    trees
and recharging with lowered blades into the root-stained loam.
Now I remembered counting earthdiggers on my fingertips in
    the sun.
Savagely they encircled me while I stood petrified and alone.
It is then I should have spoken within that snarling ring of fire
and asked myself what else I might have done.
Now I could hear the long green Euclids screaming still.
They were building a parkway through my shattered skull.

One can have a vision, but no vision is worth anything if one is too
sick to implement it. If I had to pick a poem that would initially help
me show the effect of a psychiatric intervention on my creativity, it
would be "The Euclids." The first of four poems that started with the
same opening refrain, "I was mugged," it was written a few years after
I had jumped out of a four-story hospital window, in 1966, in Aix-en-

Provence, France. I was later clinically diagnosed as suffering from schizophrenia, but now that I look at it, this act was only one more step in an accumulating mental disorder, unforeseen at the time, as I tried to find some firm ground I could stand on as a poet and a beginning writer.

My wife, Françoise, and I, and our three young daughters were living in Brooklyn, in the hard-core inner city then, in a mostly black and Puerto Rican neighborhood. Perhaps I can say that this poem reliably demonstrates to a certain degree the shattering impact of a life we were trying to put back together again. After a couple of months of confinement in the Hôpital de la Conception in Marseille—the hospital, I later found out, where the French poet Rimbaud had died—I was flown back to the United States in a half-body cast accompanied by my family.

Although I wasn't in the military then, upon returning, I was first admitted into a VA hospital. This was to give me a unique perspective on the Vietnam war years. Still, I had not only the crippling effects of my own mental condition to deal with but also, although I learned to walk again, a physical disability that was to handicap me for the rest of my life. I had fractured a couple of vertebrae in my back and, among other things, was paralyzed below the knees.

But as "The Euclids" shows, especially in the last four or five lines, and in a rage and anger not always of my choosing, there was to be an unexpected merging between my illness, the inner city, the turbulence of my youth, and, always under intense scrutiny, my own desire to write.

This, along with a manageable psychiatric intervention, which I will describe later, was eventually to engender the first real spark of hope.

DURING ONE OF MY PERIODS of hospitalization, I was transferred from King's County Hospital in Brooklyn to a more upscale private hospital in Manhattan. To this day I'm not sure who or what external power intervened for me to make this possible because, when it was necessary, one was usually transferred from King's County to a state hospital.

In one sense, because I handle medication poorly, I might have been temporarily better off at King's County, since I had managed to forestall the doctor's giving me any. My argument was quite simple and not without its own logic. Originally, I had been admitted to the old civilian-military hospital in Aix-en-Provence, from which I jumped because I had taken an overdose of a prescribed medication. I knew how I could react to drugs, and I was terrified of them.

I am not trying to deny in any way how ill I really was. But when I arrived at that new hospital, this argument did me no good. I was almost immediately placed on an extremely high dose of Thorazine. Later, I was told by a VA doctor that this was four times the legal limit in a VA hospital. Then, as now, I see no justification for this. I had been of no overt danger to anyone but myself, although I would be the first to admit that one can never exclude this possibility.

Cut off from my own sensory apparatus, upon which I rely so crucially, especially for the writing, and more convinced than ever that I was a "monster," I fell even farther into the most mentally isolated and terrifying existence. Now that I look at it, another highly questionable thing happened here. The psychiatrist told me more than once that if I had a family and wanted to write, I should do it in my spare time. "A person like you should be on Wall Street. You went to Dartmouth," she said. "When did you start on the long way down?"

Was this a Freudian slip referring to my own unfortunate exit from a window? Of course, any writing other than a few small fragments was impossible under these conditions. Françoise complained many times about the almost incoherent stupor I was in, but nothing was done to adjust my medication until she threatened to sue the hospital. It was then cut in half.

She was also told by a social worker that, because I would always be ill, it would be better if she and the children separated from me. This seemed only to intensify her resistance. She declined, as both she and my father had done when they were asked to sign a paper permitting the doctors to give me electric shock.

> My soul is sultry
> like an ill wind
> blown inland from the shore
> and carrying the stench of the dead;
> My soul is sultry
> like a whore
> the price of her body is worth
> more than she gets.

I don't know if I'll ever be able to clearly define the effect of a psychiatric intervention on my creativity. Rather, it seems as if I will always be talking about before and after I fell from the window. And since then, in an attempt to perfect this art, I have kept right on falling toward some mystery inside myself.

But for the sake of comparison, I would prefer to return to that time, in the fall of 1964, when we left for France on that potentially fatal trip.

We were living in a railroad flat in Brooklyn Heights, a fairly fashionable neighborhood overlooking the bay. Since Françoise had a degree in engineering from France, we felt that it would be easier for her to get work there and that I would have more time to write.

I had previously lost my job in the art book department of McGraw-Hill, just at the time when our second child, Gilda, was about to be born. I was working at a number of different part-time jobs in order to help support the family and still be able to concentrate on the writing. The jobs were the usual run-of-the mill things a beginning writer goes through: doorman at a hospital in uptown Manhattan; unloading furniture in a warehouse down near the docks at night for a large department store; assistant in a local Swedenborgian bookshop, etc. Françoise was also running the French School of the Heights out of our home, and later she did some teaching in a private school.

I didn't really have much to go on as a writer, and following in my father's footsteps in my inability to support my family, and without realizing it fully, I probably had a deeply rooted sense of failure. Although my father eventually did work for a small public relations firm in New York City, he was basically just a talented small-town newspaperman who, in terms of his own writing, always felt he could have done more. He also had problems with alcohol.

I don't think I realized, either, increasing in severity as it did, that I had the complications of a disease to deal with. I remember thinking, when we finally did leave New York on that Norwegian freighter, *The Black Tern,* and as we passed under the Verrazano Bridge, which was still under construction, that I would either return dead or as a successful writer.

STILL, A BEGINNING WRITER can have his moments of redemption and even a kind of heroism that, like first love, can never be experienced again. There is so much fear and insecurity to be confronted, along with optimism and excitement at the act of discovery. One can also be deluded into thinking one can challenge death, without realizing the implications. Because I was so unskilled as a writer, and in order to free myself and get the kind of inner psychic connection I wanted, I devised a method of working directly from dreams. I found that I could train myself to remember my dreams, and even enhance them by eating certain foods before I went to bed. At other times, I could be extremely punitive toward myself—which I would never advise anybody to do. Perhaps I was only answering to my own particular circumstances and needs.

Much of that writing is either lost now, or displaced, but this was an extremely effective, if dangerous, thing to do. I found that shortly after waking, and without my usual literary impediments, I could take the psychic energy from the dream world and let it, almost on its own, translate itself into short abstract sketches directly through my hand. The fascination of this was that I didn't even need the whole dream, only some salient feature whose unconscious force, uninhibited, I could provide an outlet for.

What I didn't realize was that I was also starting to unplug, and be subjected to, almost like a volcano, the vast destructive forces of a subterranean psychic energy that we all possess. Call it one aspect of the collective unconscious, if you wish, or just the blind energy of matter. And this without the least bit of knowledge or training as to how to handle it. Or even transform it. I believe a lack of discipline like this costs the lives of many artists, and probably others as well.

If there was one difference characteristic of my writing and my creativity before and after psychiatric intervention, it was the ability to tap into some of these blind channels of energy and turn, like an experienced acrobat or a fish in water, to get out of them before I got hurt. This also enabled me to examine some of the more dangerous aspects of the mind. Below is a rather humorous piece from that earlier period of writing, typical of a style and a self-imposed mode of learning I was to retain for some time.

THE TOOTH

I took my boy to the dentist. He strapped him in the chair. He set his feet against the base and picked up a pair of pliers. Music was playing over the radio as he got a good hold. He yanked and held up the tooth.

"A beauty!"

"Let's see."

He set it on a chrome platter. I could see clearly the root. It was covered with blood and had almost been penetrated by decay. I picked up a silver instrument and turned it over. The front was like a molar.

"Doc," I said. "Come here."

"What?" He was staunching the blood. He told my son to bite down hard and came over.

It was crawling with people. Some of them wore knee pants and alpine caps. A man was parading on the edge of the cavity with a tuba.

"Don't you think it's a bit unusual?"

"Not at all." He straightened his glasses. "It happens every day."

He took me over to a showcase. In it were teeth of every variety. He took out a front one and shook it.

"This one's my favorite."

"No kidding?"

Little oriental heads started popping out all over. Apparently they had been sleeping. I followed the walk of a girl in a kimono. She turned and looked at me over her umbrella.

"She's good-looking."

"Indeed she is." He put the tooth back in the showcase a little jealously.

We walked back to where my son was sitting. He lifted the gauze from his mouth and examined the wound. It had stopped bleeding.

"How does it look?"

"I could never be a dentist," I said.

I began also to live within the dream world, with its strange and uncanny abilities of prediction. This can be exhilarating, if risky. I would dream something and within a few days or a week, it would happen. The "it" could be something as small as fluid dropping from a vending machine in the Holland Tunnel and missing the cup.

Of course, one can see here a mind in the process of disintegrating. Eventually, this process was to transform itself into the shadowy incubus or succubus that perched on the back of my neck, as an actuality, when I fell from the window.

GRACE

Speak not about it.
Describe neither the place nor incident.
Silence.
Don't run the risk of poetry.
Never forget it.

If one could be cured of his own personal hell by going to hell, this would be a pretty good definition of our stay in the inner city, or "ghetto," which roughly spanned the years 1968–74. We were practically the only "white" family in the neighborhood, but it would be presumptuous of me to say that I benefited from someone else's pain and suffering. And yet I still firmly believe, as a mentally ill outcast, that this short experience on the other side of America's great "color divide" contributed substantially to my getting better. I was called upon to bear witness, especially in my first book, *Subway Prayer and Other Poems of the Inner City,* to a suffering that was not only equal to but, in many cases, far greater than my own.

I also was very lucky. I had repeatedly been diagnosed as schizophrenic, and none of the drug therapies tried on me had worked. In fact, they seemed to make my condition worse. Françoise had found a job teaching in a Quaker school, and my days at home alone were spent with skeletons hanging in the closet and blood running from people's mouths. If I went outside, the buildings and stoplights rushed up at me and receded at will. Without fanfare I had been escorted from the dream world into the world of the chronically mentally ill.

Fortunately, almost in a vision, and perhaps because our third child was on the way, I knew I couldn't stay in this condition. Suddenly, I understood that the head was attached to the body, and if I couldn't be cured, there was a message here. At least in my prayers, I could ask to learn how to "cope" with this disease.

With Françoise's help, I began to research my illness. We eventually were able to obtain a paper published in a New England medical journal by the Nobel Prize winner Dr. Linus Pauling, entitled "The Orthomolecular Treatment of Schizophrenia." I also read sources that spoke of a Dr. Abram Hoffer, a pioneer in this same treatment. About that time, by one of those inexplicable coincidences, I was referred to Dr. William Douglas Hitchings, now deceased, who was a Canadian psychiatrist practicing in New York. He was also an orthomolecular physician.

A rather generously overweight man, Dr. Hitchings was one of the kindest and most thoughtful psychiatrists I had ever met. He was also the first one who didn't treat me like a criminal. This meant a lot to me because, at certain points during my illness, I became convinced that I had participated in the assassination of Robert Kennedy, as well as others. I had also somehow become involved with Charles Whitman (a poetic reference?) in the shooting of a number of people from a campus tower at the University of Texas.

At first I didn't believe him, but Dr. Hitchings very patiently explained to me that I had a biochemical disorder that was probably genetically predisposed and that by following a niacin-based orthomolecular therapy, I could learn how to control it. Perhaps a major psychological turning point came when he asked me what I really wanted to do in life and I said I wanted to continue writing, just as I was doing. He then asked me if my wife could work, and when I said yes and added she loved to, he replied to my great relief, "Then let her. You go home and write. A person like you will never make it in business."

I think Dr. Hitchings sensed, too, that I had a vision and that there was no way out of its urgency except to confront it. Progressively over the next months and even years, I was freed from a hallucinatory world that had periodically haunted me since I was about eighteen. If it didn't disappear immediately, it gradually reduced itself to a point at which, no longer fearing it, I could control it. It was as though a dark noxious cloud that had been poisoning my brain was starting to be lifted from my mind. That shadowy entity hidden behind every corner and ready to jump out at any given moment just wasn't there.

The orthomolecular therapy also left me free to embrace my creativity with virtually no side effects, which was very important to me.

TO MY DAUGHTER, CECILE

Many are the mirrors of my mind
in which I stare
and lame as I am
I could not love you more
as you go through your ballet lesson
behind your instructor
and twist your feet
the same way I trip over words.

I had a vision of New York City and the subway, but no vision, as I have said, is worth anything if one is too sick to implement it. Whether this vision has any validity or whether I succeeded in achieving it, even partially, I will have to leave it for others to judge. I do know the vision was engraving itself on the surface of my skin even before we left for Europe in 1964, before my "accident." And as I lay close to death in the hospital in Marseille, I was convinced that I was in a subway station, looking down from my elevated perch on the people waiting on the platform.

Fortunately, that train didn't come in, although I understand more fully its meaning now. And it did manage to incorporate itself into my long poem "Subway Prayer," dedicated to Françoise, of which I give you only the opening prayer and part of another.

Our Father lost forever underground.
Our Father forever hurtling through sight and sound.
Our Father forever lurching with a drunken throat.
Our Father forever consorting with the Holy Ghost.

> Our Father forever snarling with his wicked fangs.
> Our Father forever slashing deeply with his sunken teeth.
> Our Father forever lashing painfully with a screaming harlot's
>   tongue.
> Our Father forever twisting seductively with his long metallic
>   body.
> Grant us the beauty of eternal wisdom.
> Grant us the kindness of eternal peace.

I have often wondered who the Father was I was crying out to here. Was it my own father, about whom, after I fell from the window, I kept mumbling in a delirium, "My Father was a commuter," so often that the doctors finally asked Françoise what I was talking about? Was it some hidden, ruthless face of the gods of the Old and New Testaments that, for their own good reasons, my parents had walked away from? or only the beginning point in some long transitional poem that sought to derive, from my own suffering and that of others, some common vehicle of praise?

> Our Father who takes us screaming into the darker
>   neighborhoods.
> Our Father who slashes like a silver knife through the flirting
>   stations.
> Our Father who penetrates where we do not go for fear.
> Our Father who purifies every layer of the dirt-caked girders.
> Our Father who caresses every form slouched against the
>   darkened walls.
> Our Father who knows by heart every letter of the blood-red
>   graffiti.
> Our Father who dares to stop where we do not.
> Our Father who knows the passage from dark into light.
> Our Father who knows the voyage from despair into hope.
> Our Father who knows the human soul can never have any
>   color.
> Our Father who doesn't fear the great elongated stations of our
>   darker brothers.
> Grant us freedom from the hatred of our skins.
> Grant us liberty from the division of our hearts.

The "Subway Prayer" literally exploded under my feet, as did "The Euclids," which I mentioned at the beginning of this essay, and many other poems of that period. To simplify the matter, if I had to pick one other poem that showed the effect of a psychiatric intervention on my creativity, it would be "The Glass Slipper." It contains the seeds of all I ever wanted to say in a poem, or would want to say.

THE GLASS SLIPPER

Only the soul can walk in glass slippers.
Only the soul can slip its toe into the blown glass
shaped like a bottle.
Only the soul can walk up and down on the earth
like lovers.
Only the soul can know death and live.
Only the soul can resist the bulldozer's teeth
and the journey between kingdoms.
Only the soul has a glass buckle which is chipped.
Only the soul doesn't ask why the poet has buried
the slipper with his fantasy.
Only the soul knows the lover can give no answer.

Written during our last and final stay in Brooklyn, it demonstrates, along with the "Subway Prayer" and many other poems, how a successful therapeutic intervention freed me to interpret my reactions to the inner city, using the oral or incantatory language of the streets. It also demonstrates a profound psychological change. I am firmly convinced, had I not found a reliable means of "coping" with my disease, any further writing would have been out of the question. And I probably would not have survived.

TAKING TIME OUT

Do you remember
the madness of orange trees in Venice?

How over the dikes and valleys they hung
full ready to crash to the ground.

And before the long start of the fall, seeping up from the sea,
the miles of yellow mud split-level?

And then at noon, cultivated from the lips with no more than
a yell,
the water came crashing through the poorly-constructed walls?

In the ground, the black fruit taking seed?

THOMAS KRAMPF

It is now more than thirty years since Françoise and I and the children moved to an old farm in the Allegany Mountains, near where my father's family, of German and Irish stock, took root in western rural New York. We are far from Brooklyn, but as I might have said, through the process of writing I continue to fall, with "the inner city," toward some mystery inside of myself.

In fact, if it had not been for my family and the random violence we all experienced on that block, regardless of one's color, I probably would never have left. A first-generation southern Italian, my mother was born in the city and grew up in Brooklyn. As a youth, I often visited my grandparents there.

At the same time, while I would never claim to be entirely "well," looking back on it, I hope that the "dark seed" of the experience of mental illness has borne fruit. I still have to follow a niacin-based orthomolecular regime to stabilize my frail system, and while I have never been hospitalized again, I recognize this as a possibility, should I do anything to radically affect or alter my biochemistry.

Psychologically speaking, perhaps the closest I have come to being ill again is in dredging up material for this essay and being forced to confront things I'd much rather forget. And as much as I have tried to soften this account, for my own benefit as well as the reader's, I have found it at times to be almost unbearable.

Still, I am happy to have the privilege of deriving a certain solitude from nature, and reaching a reconciliation inside myself I might not have reached. Other than the *Subway Prayer* book, I have published three additional books of poetry, the most recent of which, *Taking Time Out: Poems in Remembrance of Madness,* has allowed me to reflect on my own condition, but from a distance.

In attempting to perfect this art of falling, I believe that a successful psychiatric treatment also made possible another type of poem. Contemplative in nature, it lies in direct contrast to the incantatory style of the city poems. Perhaps it is also the result of moving to the country, but I hope that, when these poems of solitude and meditation are collected, and perhaps even published, they will, in their own small way, help to show a continuing gratitude and respect for life.

GROUND COVER

Drawing blood
my illness intensifies itself
a hybrid in the sun

It is when left alone
to surrender in the darkness
its briars

It becomes, blossoming
above the rocks, below
them beyond

The gentlest flower
in my garden.

Five

MY NAME IS NOT ALICE

REN POWELL, MA

"I'm afraid I ca'n't put it more clearly," Alice replied, very politely, "for I ca'n't understand it myself, to begin with; and being so many different sizes in a day is very confusing."

ALICE, IN WONDERLAND

My ego inflates and deflates more often than the Caterpillar's lungs as he sucks on his hookah. Although my therapist tells me not to get hung up on a diagnosis, the term for my condition is rapid cycling. Bipolar. Mixed state. Rapid cycling.

"One side will make you grow taller, the other side will make you grow shorter."

"One side of what? The other side of what?" thought Alice to herself.

"Of the mushroom," said the Caterpillar.

What I wouldn't give for Alice's mushroom. Control. Swings on demand.

I've tried lithium, homeopathy, diabetic diets, yoga, chiropractic treatments, tricyclic antidepressants, SSRIs, SNRIs, NDRIs, anticonvulsants, acupressure, light therapy, St. John's Wort, primal screaming, and excessive servings of salmon. Not to mention seven therapists, one of whom fell asleep during a session. After two years of seeing Dr. B., I received copies of his notes: he'd meticulously documented whether I'd brushed my hair before each appointment. Little else. At least the good-looking anthropology student who infiltrated my circle of college friends to do a case study had documented my more colorfully manic, "goal-oriented" activities.

During all this, I wrote: poetry, plays, essays, confessions, accusations, rambling letters, and disjointed emails. Not that I can prove it.

I threw things away. In my more dramatic moments, I burned them. Really.

And then there are the things I wish I'd burned—the manic formulations I scribbled as fast as I could and mailed off to publishers.

WINTER PORTRAIT WITH MIRROR

Her mouth is a tiny, ever-blossoming
like January's stupid, green leaves
(rushing, rushing the whole damn process)

Despite the horror stories I can tell of my experiences in the realm of psychiatry and psychoanalysis, I believe trial and error leads to success. Or at least gains. I've published two books of poetry. I don't think it's a coincidence that both of these were completed while I was taking medication. Does that mean I'd be a more prolific writer if I weren't bipolar? If I try to answer that I'm forced to ask myself whether, in that case, I'd have become a writer at all.

It's a hapless question, a bit like asking, "If you had your life to live over again . . . " And yes, people have asked if I'd choose to be bipolar. It's funny that, despite years of working with an excellent therapist on the subject of taking responsibility for my choices, including the choice to medicate, the only answer I can give is that I'm so glad it's not my choice to make.

Maybe when it's all over I can ask my children if they think the days of dancing in the kitchen were worth the days I spent shut away in the bedroom. Medication, when I did find combinations that worked, most often muted the extremes of my emotional scale. It curbed my exuberance just as it curbed the self-loathing that made me consider suicide. I found, and find, inspiration for poetry at the edges of that emotional continuum. When I'm on medication I do sometimes miss the fuzzy hallucinations and emotional highs. And yet, without the clarity that medication has afforded me, I don't think I could write the poems.

ON NOT REPEATING MYSELF

Once, in Ohio, an infant spoke to me
in the Eiffel Tower of King's Island—
the Anti-Christ leered from over his mother's shoulder.

I didn't hear him and I said
something hip, like,
"Come again?"

REN POWELL

He refused to repeat himself.
It was for the best.

All this to say:

There is this crazy bird,
a girl in cartoon prison garb,
perches on my footboard
two, three times a year—

I gave her the key
to the box
with all your letters.

One painful truth about being bipolar is that I can't excuse my manic behavior by saying "I wasn't myself." My true self is all over the place. I am myself when I hear voices and I am also myself when I am balanced, centered, with or without the help of medication. Medication doesn't change who I am; it simply keeps me in one place for a longer stretch of time. Being here is as vital to my creativity as being anywhere else on the continuum.

The catchphrase for creativity now seems to be "thinking outside the box," but there's more to it than that. I looked up *creative* in the little *Oxford American Dictionary* I keep on my desk:

Creative (kri-ay-tiv) adj. 1. having the power or ability to create things. 2. showing imagination and originality as well as routine skill, creative work.

It's the routine skill that concerns me here. When I slide out toward the edges of my continuum, it's the routine skill that suffers. I don't think that imaginative ideas without craftsmanship are artistic.

I know this is a hotly contested proclamation. I belong to a virtual community of writers, and this issue comes up regularly. There are those who hold that the true artist is not only allowed but obligated to indulge in excesses, to ignore loyalties and responsibilities for the sake of "art." The artist isn't responsible for consequences.

Ah, the myth of the inspired artist: the great poet who is to be forgiven for his (yes, traditionally, *his*) blatant flouting of all rules of relationships: the artist as possessed, demigod-like, and irreproachable in his honesty. Ask any teenage girl what it means to love a poet and she'll tell you, *wistfully,* about the inevitability of being burned. A romantic aura of suffering surrounds the poet. The artist is expected to do wrong. Transgress the Polite.

I'm jumping octaves again
Startling pigeons in front of the cathedral

Trolling the lake's edge
Sending swans huffing into the reeds
(Once I caught them eating the ducklings and they've never
    forgiven me)

The catfish suck at the high notes
Percussive smacks of mistake

No, I sing, no, I sing, no

Put my nipples under the loupe
You'll find clusters of taut-skinned cloudberries

Wear my diaphragm for a hat
And I'll sing you into the asphalt.

Not surprisingly, there's an enormous amount of literature online, literary and otherwise, regarding creativity and mental illness. A good deal of it is published by people with bipolar disorder themselves. The Internet is our candy store. The world at your fingertips is instant gratification. And true to the nature of the bipolar person, it's also instant humiliation and instant wreckage.

There are chat rooms and bulletin boards praising depression as the source of all art. Manic self-promotion with an attitude of, "This IS TRUE ART; fuck coherency." This kind of ranting is comforting to read when your are faced with rejection slips that demand that you catch the difference between *beat* and *beet* and take the time to run a spell check. I find the lists of posthumous diagnoses particularly amusing. Thinking that I have something in common with Virginia Woolf, Vivian Leigh, and even Abraham Lincoln is, well, flattering. A kind of shared quality that means I am also destined for greatness, for a romantically tragic fate. It's a seductive thought.

For the last ten years I've been teaching high school: drama, of all things. A couple of years ago I experienced side effects while weaning from a medication; I was confused and dizzy much of the time. I've never been secretive about being bipolar. I've never been secretive about my penchant for red onions and cheese on toast, either. But it had never been appropriate or necessary to discuss these things in the classroom. However, finding myself literally stumbling through Movement for Stage classes and seeing the concern on the students' faces, I decided to tell them I was experiencing some temporary side effects from a medication.

"Are you all right? What are you taking medication for?"

"I'm fine. It's for bipolar disorder."

No one gasped. In fact, little changed in the classroom. What did happen? My poetry books had been in the school's library for three years, but only now were my students checking them out. Going to the bookstore and buying copies for me to sign. While I thought that I was doing my share to debunk people's preconceptions of mental illness (after working in this small town for so many years I'd proved I was a competent and reliable teacher, a bit moody perhaps, but professional nonetheless), my *confession* may have done nothing but reinforce the idea that artistic talent and mental illness go hand in hand. Since I was teaching at a performing arts school, my classes made up of young, aspiring actors, this was worrisome. It was obvious that, in their eyes, my mental disorder gave me clout as an artist.

Many of my students are "dramatic" by nature. This is no surprise. What is surprising to me, still, is how many people, especially parents, interpret this kind of sensitivity as a choice. An affectation. A character flaw. No wonder emotional people want to be acknowledged as artists, because only then will the measure of their subjective experiences be accepted as genuine. The artist has the right to feel deeply the most mundanely inspired emotions. The rest of us are "putting on," "wallowing," and should "snap out of it." I'm not denying that some people are intentionally hyper-emotive in their quests for attention, but it is a cruel assumption to make about any individual's behavior. In our society we're terribly ambivalent when it comes to emotions. We admire suffering and martyrdom while condemning emotional demonstrations as a sign of weakness and indulgence. The artist, however, is allowed, even encouraged, to break with convention. This includes being overtly emotive.

SINGING LESSONS

most people can't sing
because they've been taught
not to scream.
But at the central tendon of her diaphragm,
a tiny frond begins to unfurl—
white now,

like this morning's haze
over the sea and the woods.
But its greening will pierce
the membrane of civility.

The artist deviates from the norm. His or her insanity is proof of deviation: the extraordinary mind. Of course, I was aware of the Sylvia Plath effect and had avoided mentioning that I was bipolar to colleagues for fear of being regarded as a posturing amateur: I am mentally unbalanced, ergo, a serious artist. When I look back now and evaluate the wisdom in "coming out" to my students, when I question my motives, I am satisfied that it was within the context of explaining my use of medication to address their concerns.

Although I'm not aware of any official name for it, I believe there is such a thing as the Charles Bukowski effect, and it's just as insidious as the Sylvia Plath effect. Bukowski's insistence that the "writer needs something to write about," coupled with his own determination to live on the edge of society as an alcoholic and transient (or at least doing his best to foster this aspect of his own myth), sets a dangerous example: the more socially abhorrent, the more artistic; the more severe the mental disturbance, the greater the creative ability. No need even to begin to discuss Sartre's hagiography of Jean Genet.

I don't agree with the portrait of the poet-as-degenerate. I don't want to be a part of promoting it. Pompous as it may be to articulate, teaching carries with it the obligation of providing students with a role model. My students found out that I'm bipolar. That I'm a poet. They also know that I'm a mother and a responsible adult who takes medication when necessary and without shame. No, I'm not saying I write as well as Bukowski or Plath, but I'm not dead. I may yet write a masterpiece.

Out of all the writers I know personally (people who make a living writing) none of them is bipolar. At least not that I know of. When it comes to publishing, I assume it's like any business, and mental illness is not seen as an advantage. It's not something an established, serious writer puts on his or her CV.

I've met a lot of people who've told me about experiences with people with bipolar disorder that had left them wary. A wonderful babysitter picked up on my mood swings in the time it took me to drop off and pick up my son each day. We got along well, but she kept me at arm's length. Could be that she just didn't like me very much. It could also be that her father was bipolar and had hurt her many times over the years—so much so that she no longer had contact with him. He was a writer. Was. Her father isn't dead. He is an alcoholic and was a writer. His publishers have given up on him and he is now unemployed and unproductive. A cautionary tale.

If I have any success at all as a writer it is as much despite my disorder as because of it. For every right turn great leaps of imagination have awarded me, I made a wrong turn because of my mania. I was once invited to make a speech at the annual meeting of the Norwegian Journalists' guild. It was an honor and could have done wonders for my career. As it was, I was hypomanic and turned up completely unprepared, rattling on without an outline or notes of any kind, but feeling immense: I was Alice in Wonderland, my arms reaching through the windows, my left hand on the coast of England, my right on the Great Wall of China.

After this, I went back on medication for a while.

A TRIP TO THE ORIENT

Setting up fences to contain the mania that comes every fall. Walking the perimeter. Had a question for you yesterday, but realized as I walked around *Breivatnet* for the second time that I had had too much wine that night to remember your studio door. I remember the hedgehog in the taxi's headlights, waddling naked past my front gate when I got home— thinking that I hadn't even tasted what was offered, wondering if that really was a virtue. (Because I have so few, I collect them like art.) Relishing the seldom high tide of wanting. But in all the remembering, I forgot the question and went to the quay instead and watched the fish jumping.

Years ago, after I was first diagnosed, I read a book by the actress Patty Duke. She talked about lithium and how it had saved her life. She called it her magic pill. I'm lithium-resistant, but the time I spent taking the drug was productive in my treatment. Because my dosage was high, I had to watch my intake of caffeine and alcohol, as well as any signs of hypomanic or manic behavior. I began the habit of self-monitoring. I learned to predict situations that would push me toward the extremes and to develop the discipline it takes to avoid them. Self-monitoring is an endurance sport. It's exhausting holding all the fences in place, while watching my feet and holding my tongue at the same time: *stay within the boundaries.* I am still developing that discipline.

I also began looking at my writing as a private diagnostic tool. Keeping a journal and reading the previous night's entry helped me be objective about my mental state. Paranoia is extraordinarily vivid in journal entries, even when you're only distanced by twenty-four hours. Sometimes the handwriting itself reveals volumes.

A LOVE STORY

So she grates this time
over the keyboard, circumcising her fingertips with the blunt instrument,
getting around the loops too narrow, or those
     wide
         enough to fit
            the fat lady singing her Arias
           right
              through
full stops *andintothoseearlyhoursofthenight:*
        tot's ear   our soft hen,
          Oh, Lover, how I
      wish we'd had that baby
     that slipped between my labia all
             too soon
         sugar-coated candy chick   *she'd be two now*
                           chirping and squawking and
                           molting that soft,
                           Easter yellow for blood-
                           y pairing
                           you dick.

And twelve years later,
an e-mail. No sarcasm:
He misses her
hand-written poems.

Four years ago, my doctor and I did find a combination of medication that worked fairly well: Depakote and Effexor. It was also during this time that I found a therapist whom I respected and who focused on the present instead of the past. It was a good combination for me. I remained on medication for nearly two years and began writing fearlessly for the first time in my life: that is, I began *editing* with confidence. And publishing more regularly. And yet one of the side effects I had to endure was drowsiness. I was sleeping twelve or more hours a day, experienced continuous lethargy and weight gain, and my spouse was stuck with 100 percent of the housework while I napped. When I complained to my psychiatrist he said he wouldn't condone "playing with medications" and that the combination I had was "good enough." He also stressed that it wasn't appropriate for me to be trolling the Internet and coming in to request specific medications. Stopping medication was a difficult decision, but I felt I had no choice.

The following two years without medication were tolerable, but not pleasant. I wrote and I became involved with an activist group, which provided me with the opportunity to travel. However, not surprisingly, traveling brought on hypomania.

I began to fear that the manic behavior would cost me the chance to work with the NGO, which was personally and professionally satisfying—or worse, that it would cost me my marriage. I began weighing again the pros and cons of medication. I thought to give lithium another try. It wasn't working, and I felt a depressive episode clawing at my ankles. Then, when going to a private clinic for an unrelated problem, I met a moonlighting neurologist who scribbled *Lamictal* on a slip of paper and told me to read up on it. I did. I called her back, and she started me on the schedule of increasing dosages while I waited for an appointment she'd made for me with a colleague she respected.

My current psychiatrist functions as my therapist as well. I've been on the therapeutic dosage for only three months now, and I am trying to suppress the hope that this is *my* magic pill. One day it struck me that I'd gone a whole week without snapping at my children. I'd gone a whole week without the noise in my head. No mental self-flagellating. No tirades about my colleague's incompetence. And I've been writing.

My new doctor has no need to play the gatekeeper of magic potions and even says that, if the medication continues to work, we will discuss how I can regulate the dosage without having to come in to see her every time there's a bump in the road. After twenty-one years of consciously struggling with the ups and downs, after experiencing the extremes—for good and for not-at-all-good—I can't let myself think I've really found Alice's mushroom. But if it works for a while, at least I will have a stretch of peace in which to be truly creative.

Six

MY OLDEST VOICE

JESSE MILLNER, MFA

WHEN I VISIT MY THERAPIST on Monday mornings, late in my life, here in bizarre and beautiful south Florida, I talk about guilt. I tell her about my shame over being a bad Baptist kid who could never accept Jesus, my guilt over my failed first marriage, and a blue-collar life in Chicago. I talk about the misery of fifteen years of drinking, and oddly enough, I talk about the guilt I've felt over twenty years of sobriety, and how, even though the booze is gone, I still hate myself and feel tremendous sadness and am still depressed. I tell her I feel guilty for taking Prozac, which seems to be helping but feels like cheating.

WHEN I FIRST BEGAN WRITING poems as a freshman at the University of Virginia in 1971, I fueled the process with booze, depression, and an acute longing for a girlfriend. I believed that if I wrote poems that showed my heartbreaking loneliness, along with my incredible sensitivity, women would chase me down the halls of my dorm. So I drank, listened to depressing music, and wrote from that place of sorrow I'd always cultivated but could more easily reach with beer and bourbon.

Unfortunately, I wrote really bad poems, and women ran the other way. But the cycle of drinking, depression, and creativity carried on. Alcohol took me to the darkest, saddest places, and I loved being wherever I ended up. After fifteen years of drinking, after reaching that point where I simply couldn't drink and continue to live, I went into a treatment facility that helped save my life. I worried that without booze, I would no longer be able to write. I discovered that I could still write because, even without liquor, I was incredibly depressed. And I could write from that forlorn, dejected state, I could still plunge myself into darkness and thus be able to generate poems from that melancholy I loved so much.

March 6, 1986 at Chicago's Alcoholic Treatment Center, 26th and California, adjacent to the Cook County Jail:
Was very depressed over the weekend. Have rapid mood swings, hyperactivity, nervousness, inability to concentrate, difficulty in falling asleep, fear about facing the "outside world," because I realize I'll have the same problems I had before when I leave here.

When I look at my journal from the treatment days, I hear my voice struggling to be heard over depression and the withdrawal from alcohol. In many ways the treatment center was a horrible place. I shared a cubicle with four other men. One of them had just gotten out of prison and the other three had chosen treatment over jail. The view to the north out of our grated window revealed the Cook County Jail complex, with its guard towers and walls crowned with barbed wire. At first I felt out of place and frightened of that place and the people I shared it with. But gradually I realized that many of these men suffered from the same problems as I: depression and alcoholism and/or drug addiction. I wrote every day in the treatment center. I wrote overly sentimental poems about my suffering:

Watching jailhouse shadows,
new brick reflections,
and hell behind the architect's dream.
An opposite sacred place,
condemned by brutal men
on brutal men. It lives
as well in heat as indifferent snow.

Yuk! But when I read these lines I remember so clearly the way I felt that March in Chicago, when I finally turned away from booze and looked for other ways to deal with my depression. And somehow I knew that writing would keep me alive.

Through the years of sobriety I found myself writing poems. Ironically, I think it was because that deep well of sadness that I'd written from when I was drinking was still inside me. I was sober but I was depressed. Removing alcohol from my life had helped, but it hadn't relieved that basic sorrow that had always been a part of me.

I haven't had a drink for twenty years. However, until last winter, I hadn't faced my depression. I thought I needed it to write. But more than that, I believed I needed it to live. Oftentimes I'd find myself withdrawing from my life, closing my office door at work, retreating to an unoccupied room in my house so that I could crawl into depression and feel the relief, the absence of anxiety that would come from "getting low."

Finally, last February, I decided to get help and went to see a psychiatrist. He prescribed Prozac and promised it would bring relief. To augment the medication, I began seeing a therapist last spring. And in May, at a writing residency in Wyoming, the darkness began to lift.

WHEN I FIRST STARTED taking Prozac, I worried about my writing. My mentor in graduate school, Campbell McGrath, told me once to follow the mental framework of my brain as I wrote a poem, to take those leaps that came to me in the course of composition. And for me, poetry writing has been a weird, leaping kind of thing. The best poems have been little voyages of discovery, and the worlds they've gone to have truly surprised me. I was afraid that Prozac might stifle me, inhibit those voyages, subtly change the mental structure of my brain in a way that would keep me from the wild, intuitive jump.

Similarly, when I first stopped drinking, I'd worried that my poetry would suffer. I feared I had lost my touchstone of grief and that everything I wrote would become Hallmark drivel. In each case, the first time with booze and second time with my untreated depression, I had to decide what was more important, my writing or my *life*. Nearly twenty years ago I gave up alcohol and saved my life; last winter I gave up not treating my depression and took the next step in enriching my life.

I needn't have worried. After I quit booze, my writing got better and I wrote more frequently. I started attending poetry workshops at a high school at night, and I felt the possibilities of my own work for the first time. These workshops led directly to my decision to go back to school and pursue an MFA degree in poetry. In the last two months on Prozac, I've been doing readings to support the release of my first book. I find myself enjoying the readings more and truly being present when I speak my work.

IT'S EARLY MAY in Wyoming and three feet of snow is expected. Piney Creek, just beyond my front window, is swollen and filled with debris. A wild turkey roots around on the near bank and a great blue heron stands on the far bank. There is no bridge for me to cross to reach that further shore, and the fast water will not let me pass. Two of the other residents tell me that just last week it was 70 degrees, and they were diving off the low cliff behind the residence into the cold water. There were turtles and leeches.

A stand of cottonwoods on the shore is about to become an island. A picnic table that yesterday was fifteen yards from the water is now about to float away. Where is all this water going?

I've always been afraid of water. The Baptist women taught me to fear drowning and serpents, so the worst fate, I suppose, would have been to fall into a pond full of water moccasins. As a child growing up in California, I never strayed far into the Pacific, content to build sand castles as close to the rushing current as possible. Frost used to watch his father swim in San Francisco Bay, and I used to watch my own father swim in the ocean, though he never taught me how.

Until my mother threatened to leave him, for a brief while in San Diego, my father trained to be a navy diver. Once he even brought home abalone for dinner. The meat was tough but the shell reflected back a rainbow.

I WAS ONCE A DROWNED BOY

On those cold nights when I'd first stopped
drinking, when sobriety hung by the most slender of threads,
when I'd walk past the Kuwaiti grocery on Sheffield
where during my drinking days I'd purchased
a half pint and a six pack every night on the way home,
on those frozen nights looking for the moon kept
me from staring through the frosted window
with its ads for tuna fish and laundry detergent
toward the coolers in the back of the store
filled with Old Style, Budweiser and Pabst Blue Ribbon.

Rather than dwell on that plentitude of beers,
I'd look up at the sky, seeking answers
in the swerve of yellow light
as I walked past Wrigley Field,
then the Cubby Bear Lounge at Clark and Addison
where I spent many a night in infamy,
talking to the large-breasted bartender
who hated me and my eyes swollen like sunken
moons, the kind the fishes see from under the water.

There's a ten-foot bank protecting me from Piney Creek, but the rising water still makes me nervous. The water has rushed down from the Bighorn Mountains, so I bet it's very cold and, judging from the speed of the occasional branches, moving very fast. The snow is falling heavy again as the afternoon damply comes on. But the long spring grasses continue to assert themselves, pushing through the wet snow.

I was once like those grasses, half-asleep in my torpor of alcohol and depression, the cold world sweeping over me, my brain numb behind my eyes. For years I drove a bus in Chicago, and each afternoon after work I'd wander into Charlie's on Randolph and drink myself into a daze, then climb into my '75 Pinto and drive home past Cabrini Green, then the warehouses on Clybourne. I'd get home in late afternoon and climb into bed for a nap. Our bedroom was tiny with peach walls. I'd be exhausted from getting up at 5 AM after drinking late into the night. I'd fall asleep, only to wake to strange creatures crawling across the walls and ceiling. Then I'd treat my insomnia with a couple shots of bourbon and fall back into a very troubled sleep.

AS I LOOK BACK to a particular Wednesday in January of 1985, I see myself walking past Rose Records on Ashland. I've just visited the automatic teller and punched out my password with shaking fingers. I was unable to get any money because my account was overdrawn. Now I'm walking down Cornelia on the edge of the street because the sidewalk is snow-covered and impassible. An old Buick passes me, westbound, and the driver's side window rolls down and a Styrofoam cup spins toward me, then soaks me with cold beer.

At first I get angry and start to chase the car. But then the old voice inside tells me that I deserve it, and I feel even more depressed and can't wait to get home to drink.

HERE IN WYOMING, the music blares on. It's the soundtrack of my life: "I hate you, I hate you," played by a bad country and western band at a bar at the edge of the world where angels dance with cowboys and broken-down farmers sip moonshine. At the therapist's office every two weeks, I try to understand that voice, try to ease the self-hatred that almost killed me.

The voice would follow me everywhere. In my drinking days I'd look in the mirror each morning and cuss out the face that looked back at me. "Fuck you, asshole," I whispered to the bloated apparition who was thirty years old and looked fifty. I wanted to slam my fist through the glass and smash the face.

THE ONE VOICE

the voice that dared me to drink one more drink,
the voice that asked me to open my wrist, to present

those crimson flowers to the waters

.   .   .   .

Today the wind has blown since dawn
and that voice has drowned out my own, and I'm
grateful for the High Plains' rattle and moan,

grateful for the twilight gathering in the hills,
voice of shadow and dissolution, voice of black
night in the mountains, voice of Western meadowlark at dusk.
Yesterday when I walked toward the setting sun,
and followed a squeaking killdeer toward the place
where the Bighorns swallow the last minutes of the day,
my own wild voice was forgotten
as one by one
long-dead stars punctured the sky.

Why are some of us born with that voice? I hated myself for being tall
and skinny. I hated myself because my navy father made me get those
fifty-cent haircuts at the Navy Exchange. I hated myself because my
nose was too big. I hated myself because of the acne that broke out in
seventh grade. I hated myself because my voice took two years to
change, sentencing me to a squeaky, off-key adolescence. But mostly I
hated myself because I had fallen so far short spiritually. I couldn't believe in Jesus, yet I did believe in the Big Guy who'd punish me for
every transgression. I didn't believe in heaven, but I was convinced of
the certainty of hell. That was the true gift, the real world of fundamen-
talism: that fiery burning lake awaiting those of us who could not accept Jesus as our personal savior, those of us who lied occasionally, or
cheated on a spelling test, or stole grapes at the Safeway, or looked at
pictures of naked women in a moldy *Playboy* someone had found in a
dumpster. I hated myself for the emptiness I felt each Sunday when I
couldn't accept Jesus:

ALL-STARS OF THE BIBLE

I'd sit next to my mother
in the suffocating dullness of the preacher's
words interspersed with dutiful hymns
until we finally reached the climax
when all the saved brothers and sisters marched
up to the mourner's bench,
their mouths stretched to orgasm
as I listened to the boredom whirring in my head,

and unlike Blake's terrible angels,
the notes sang neither Hell nor Paradise;
I heard the nothingness
of an empty room filled with believers
singing "Oh Lamb of God, I call."

These days I feel better. I've lived every day of my life so far with fear and sadness. I still do. But I don't feel the urge to slink deep down into sorrow and stay there. I don't want to kill myself. This very moment, Piney Creek rushes past my studio here at the residence. Fat orioles feed in the tall grass that falls down to the stream banks. As I rode my bike over here this afternoon, I saw mule deer grazing in a field alongside the road.

Wild turkeys strutted next to a stand of cottonwood trees. The deer looked up when I passed by, but didn't run. The turkeys ignored me. And as I pedaled east, I realized there was not another human in sight; I was totally alone. I turned east into the Ucross driveway and as I looked to my right, I could see the Bighorn Mountains twenty-eight miles to the north. I was alone with the deer, the turkeys, the miles of high plains and foothills stretching toward the white summits of the mountains. I was alone with the cold wind pushing me faster toward my studio. Where this window awaits. Where this laptop purrs silently, waiting for the next leap, waiting for the next journey away from sorrow.

Yesterday, I spent five hours writing about my life-long depression, even as rabbits lingered in the studio's front yard, sampling the warmth of early spring. The view out my window is spectacular—the High Plains, a swollen, snow-fed creek in the foreground. Cottonwoods greening in the flood plain. And a sky so bright it's enough to almost make me believe in God. The view outside keeps pulling me out of myself, away from the dark depths of the past. I'm writing now to find a way in, an entry point toward the territory I really want to explore. In the meantime, I look at the yellow dandelions on the bluff above the creek or check out the red-winged blackbird whose crimson is brighter than blood, otherworldly in this Wyoming morning light.

I watched television last night, a weird diversion here in the middle of nowhere, but the residency has satellite television and nine hundred stations. We watched a show where one of the characters was on Prozac and I perked up, hoping he would turn away from his phobia of bridges and live happily ever after, restored to the good life through chemistry. I'm always looking for happy Prozac stories; I want to believe that it does help, that it's not an illusion, this calmness I've felt recently.

The last two nights here, I slept all the way through, not waking until morning. Maybe it's the quiet of the High Plains and that blanket of star-pierced, yet velvet black surrounding me that helps me sleep, or maybe it is the Prozac somehow altering my brain chemistry, keeping the nightmares at bay.

On Tuesday it snowed a foot, and I walked the mile from my sleeping quarters to the studio in the raw, wet cold, only to realize I'd forgotten to take my medication, so I walked back. And in the white fields mule deer jumped over barbed-wire fences like grace itself, their bodies gaining altitude so effortlessly, I thought of angels. And the wild turkeys pecked and preened by a little creek, occasionally unfurling their tail feathers into beautiful black fans. I went back to my room and swallowed the green and white pill, then walked back to the studio, watching low clouds skim over the ragged summits of hills.

THESE DAYS I rarely think of suicide, but the voice within that reminds me I'm a piece of shit still whispers in dark moments. My experiences with AA and therapists have certainly helped, but, all this time without booze, I've still not been able to be totally honest. Here goes: I'm still depressed. I'm still in many ways the lonely little kid who craves isolation. I still enjoy being sad. Not drinking was important because it helped save my life, but sobriety alone couldn't cure the emptiness inside me, that sorrow that's always been there.

When I was asked to write this essay, I was forced to think about my depression. I wondered how I could participate in this project when therapy had not really helped, when I still felt the same sadness I'd always felt. I believed that somehow I was cheating, that I should have been able to battle this thing without medication. A search of Prozac on the Internet revealed a million voices screaming that it doesn't work. But, before I went to see the psychiatrist, I'd decided to be totally honest about my depression. I talked about everything that was going on; how, even though my life was going well, I still felt sad and anxious, I still felt as if there was something different, something unworthy, about me. I decided to trust the doctor and my therapist, and for a while to shut out the voices on the Internet and that older voice deep inside me.

I was afraid I'd lose my writing voice, that the poems wouldn't come, that I'd be somehow numb inside. After all, wasn't it the melancholy that led me to write? Hasn't sorrow always been the wellspring of inspiration for me? It helps that James Wright, late in life, turned away from booze, and his poems, like his life, came to brim with light.

RIGHT NOW I'm soothed by the High Plains, which stretch away from my window; Piney Creek in the foreground; closer still a gold-finch alights from the deck. Right now Prozac flows through my body, intervening between the bright world outside and the darker one I've cultivated my whole life.

To write poems is to venture forth constantly into the forests of the past, to walk down hills not knowing quite where they'll lead. In the pine forests of my childhood, there were still black bears gouging big caves out of the hillsides. Here in Wyoming, mountain lions live far-ther back in the hills that rise toward the Bighorns.

Yesterday I saw a dead rattlesnake on the side of the road. It was gleaming and perfect except for its crushed head. Perhaps these fields are teaming with snakes, especially that one meadow where the prairie dogs live, their black holes everywhere. I often write poems about snakes. When I was a Baptist kid, the preacher told us the story of the serpent in the garden from Genesis, and there were literal snakes in my grandmother's vegetable garden behind the henhouse: king snakes, black snakes, the occasional copperhead. I was afraid of snakes as a child, and in my poems I'm trying to see them as the beautiful creatures they are. Once while walking the Florida Trail near Kissim-mee, I saw a pair of indigo snakes emerge from a cypress slough and speed off into a tiny prairie, the kind that reminds you of the West be-cause of the high brown grasses. I often think about those snakes as I move through my daily life, the grace of their motion, the companion-able space they seemed to share as they moved through that world.

I am fifty-two years old now and still afraid of snakes. My mother made us run from every serpent we saw on those summer dirt roads, in that garden filled with yellow blooms of squash, guarded by barbed wire covered with honeysuckle. I write poems to get over my snake fear; I write poems to help me with depression.

I believe poems are prayers. My mind goes out into the world, slips into the past, worries about the future, then returns to my notebook, where the images collect like the colors of the day: brown rattlesnake, black-faced junco, yellow dandelions, May breeze, the scent of burning leaves from a nearby ranch. Robert Hass has said that images allow us to live twice, and I gather these remnants of the senses and store them in the place where my sorrow also collects. That long rain that has been falling since childhood. That sadness at the very heart of me. My shadow, my oldest voice.

Seven

HOW I LEARNED TO COUNT TO FOUR

AND LIVE WITH THE GHOSTS OF ANIMALS

VANESSA HALEY, MFA, MSW

VIRGINIA COMMONWEALTH UNIVERSITY offered me a non-tenure-track instructorship in the English Department when I was twenty-eight, and, after spending a spring and summer as a sabbatical replacement in a tiny college in western New York in the middle of the snow belt, I was glad to migrate south to warmer weather. This was my first full-time faculty position, and though I had confidence in my teaching ability, the social aspects of the job—attending faculty meetings and colleagues' parties—caused me great anxiety. In addition to teaching a grueling course load of three sections of composition and one creative writing class per semester, I began long-term psychotherapy. My obsessive-compulsive and post-traumatic stress disorder symptoms—which ranged from counting and cleaning rituals to moderate dissociation and claustrophobia—were the defense mechanisms gone awry I developed as a result of growing up with an unpredictable and sometimes violent parent. I consider them to be my first act of creativity. Had I not developed OCD and invented the elaborate rituals to ensure my own safety, surely, my magical thinking allowed me to believe, I would have been consumed by my father's rage.

The chaos of changing jobs and moving twice in one year, as well as having to share an office with a female version of my father—albeit one with a PhD degree, but equally as explosive—exacerbated my need for routine, cleanliness, and order. My apartment was immaculate, the carpet vacuumed twice a day, the spices arranged alphabetically in their small yellow McCormick tins, the bathtub scoured with Comet until the enamel lost its gleam. I lay awake ruminating about the lecture I'd prepared for a class, and when I did fall into fitful bouts of sleep, I dreamed of horses swimming across the James River, struggling against the current until they gave up and were swept away in a roar of white rapids. It was a variation of a nightmare I'd had since I was four, after my parents had taken me to the Steel Pier in Atlantic City to see "The Diving Horse."

"Four" was my magic number. Fortuitously, I had a four-year contract and a four-class course load, and I could get off the city bus four blocks from campus and walk to the architecturally uninspired building that housed the English Department. I read in the *Richmond Times Dispatch* that Richmond was ranked fourth in the nation for the number of violent crimes per capita. My fourth-floor office, which I shared with a bitter woman who resembled my fourth-grade teacher, Miss Rowe (down to her black plastic-frame glasses and bleached-blonde hair), was a fourteen-by-fourteen room crammed with two desks, a central bookcase already filled with my office mate's tomes on medieval literature, and a single IBM roller-ball Selectric typewriter, which we were supposed to share. Needless to say, I rarely got a turn on the typewriter, because Dr. Medieval was busy churning out application letters to distant universities in land-locked states, probably in the middle of the dust bowl. During her seventh year she had applied for but was denied tenure. "No offense," she said, "nothing personal, but I just don't want to talk to you or anyone else, so just leave me alone and we'll be fine." The only other remark she made to me was to let me know she did not vote for my candidacy when I interviewed for the position. "I didn't really care for your poems," she confided. "Too many dead animals."

On a few occasions I forgot her golden rule, and I asked things like, "Where do I go to get a faculty parking sticker?" or "I'm going to get a coffee, would you like me to pick one up for you?" She would stop pecking at the typewriter, take a deep breath, and with one hand, make a slashing gesture across her throat to silence me. My father used to do the same thing at the dinner table when my mother and I tried to have a conversation while he was watching a sporting event on television, angled so that he could see it from his captain's chair in the dining room. We'd whisper, "Please pass the butter . . . Want more peas?" while sideline cheerleaders, perpetually vivacious, turned cartwheels and shook their pom-poms on the glowing TV screen, and my father sat rapt in the vicarious thrill of football, yelling out profanities and slamming his hand down on the table when his team missed a field goal or fumbled the ball. If no games were televised, we ate in silence every day just before or just after four o'clock; the time depended on whether he'd worked the day or night shift at the mill located only a block from our house.

My psychologist, Frances, had an office in the west end of Richmond, not far from Monument Avenue, where equestrian statues immortalized Confederate generals Robert E. Lee, Stonewall Jackson, and J. E. B. Stuart. The original capital of the Confederacy, Richmond was burned to the ground during the Civil War and then rebuilt. The old tobacco warehouses in Shockoe Bottom were transformed into trendy restaurants and boutiques, and many sections of the city were being "gentrified." It was a city of contradictions, striving to be progressive, yet bound by its traditions. I had come south to face my own past, whether I wanted to or not. Like Richmond itself, I needed to admit that I had lost my own war with anxiety. I had to reconstruct myself. And the only way I could do that was to travel back to my past, retrieve the child I once was, and bring her back with me to a more accepting place. How could I tell my story of trauma and loss without risking the very feelings I had tried my whole life to avoid?

Writing poems and publishing them in literary journals was a safe venue. Strangers might sit in the afternoon sunlight at a university library and happen upon one of my poems by chance in a literary magazine. Poetry, when read by someone other than the poet, becomes dialectical, though anonymously so. Unlike many poets, who attend literary conferences and book public readings, I prefer to write in private and mail my poems to distant journals for editors (whom I will never meet) to read. Anonymity is comforting to someone suffering from a range of disorders in the anxiety spectrum. Sitting face to face with a psychologist, however, forces interaction. While describing my childhood during our sessions, and in turn listening to my therapist's responses, I came to realize that psychotherapy, like creativity, involves the difficult tasks of unearthing our buried life-fragments and then recognizing patterns and associations that give shape and meaning to an existence. Both undertakings are a sometimes dark, occasionally shimmering distillation that helps us move beyond recognition and insight, toward transcendence of the self and a communion with others.

There are some rare moments while I'm writing when language flows from a place I did not, just moments before, know I could access. This happens most often when I arise at two or three in the morning, knowing there will be no reprieve from my insomnia but too exhausted to do any household chores. My analytic side is somehow suppressed at this point, and I can tap into a clarity of detail that rushes all at once in brilliant flashes, as though I am shape-shifting, assuming an identity and consciousness other than my own. Creativity occurs when I allow a dissolution of self and access the primitive psychic fears and longings hovering just beyond anxiety's sharp edges, drifting to the lake's undulating bottom where *fish unfold in my consciousness like memory long submerged. I become the snapping turtle locked inside itself* with *visions of damselflies needling the air . . . with jeweled thinness . . . mildly beguiled by the glint of wavering fins . . . and light filtering through algae in vague green columns;* or the groundhog, tunneling through dry earth *to make a home: a ceiling of roots, pale tendrils . . . no light or sound . . . just the movements of moles or insects traveling blind.* Like the cicada that breaks free of one body to assume a winged version of itself, I momentarily experience the sensory perceptions of another being, transforming the fear of disintegration into the possibility of renewal through creative flight.

Much of the literature on post-traumatic stress syndrome describes various levels of dissociation as a common reaction to trauma. My psychologist asked me how connected I felt to my body. She observed that while I described some of my memories of my father's outbursts—punching a hole in the living room wall, breaking my pogo stick in half by smashing it repeatedly on the sidewalk, tossing a bowl of popcorn in my face when he got angry about a dentist bill (I had cracked a tooth on a popcorn kernel the week before)—I seemed to fall into a trance, staring into space as I spoke. Sometimes, during the therapy, I felt as though I were floating. At the beginning of my work with Frances, she permitted my mild dissociation and distancing, but eventually her task was to assist me in the integration of past and present, to help me *reexperience* (in the safety of her office) the fear, shame, and betrayal I had tried to avoid for eighteen years. When I made my weekly journey to Frances's office, I drove past Lee's equestrian statue, *his oxidized eyes . . . still searching the distance for the enemy line . . . his horse poised in a posture of near-flight.* And it occurred to me that this massive bronze image of hypervigilance, frozen fear, and inevitable defeat was a physical reminder of how my early childhood experiences had shaped my own inability to move beyond the past.

During our sessions, I recalled with stunning clarity several instances in which I saw my father killing or hurting animals. He was an avid hunter, with a collection of rifles and handguns. He packed his own shotgun shells, sitting at the dining room table, with a shell press mounted to a piece of plywood. Often, on Sunday nights, while my mother and I watched *The Wonderful World of Disney* on our black-and-white television, my father sat grooming his guns, rubbing the blue carbon steel barrels with an oily rag and polishing the walnut stocks. My father shot deer, rabbits, squirrels, doves, pheasants, quail, ducks, geese, and, as a favor to local farmers, groundhogs. He also caught and ate bullfrogs and snapping turtles.

I even saw him shoot his beagle, Bell, "because she was too old to run rabbits anymore." It was January 20, 1961, the day after my seventh birthday. The second major snow of the season had fallen all night, and the small town's team of snowplows cleared the streets, flakes whirling in the twin tunnels of amber cast by the headlights. It must have been a Saturday, since my mother wasn't home. She worked part time at a small department store. My father told me to get my boots, mittens, and coat on, because we were going for a ride. For a brief second, I felt happy; maybe he was going to take me sledding. But I watched him from the back door walk right by my sled leaning against the metal trashcans. He opened the dog pen gate and kicked at two of the beagles, letting only one of them out. She scampered and slid across the frozen crust, not making much headway, so he bent over and picked her up and carried her under one arm to the car and put her in the trunk. That's where the beagles rode when he took them rabbit hunting.

It was a 1957 two-tone Chevy, the kind with fins. The ice on the windows had already been scraped off, because he had driven my mother to Sadoff's Department Store earlier. When he drove too fast, the rear of the car fishtailed four times on icy patches, but I kept my eyes on the pristine fields blanketed in white streaking away from me in the sideview mirror. I can still see the red blur of my mitten wiping a path through the steam my breath made on the car window, then morphing into the red snow fences farmers had rolled out to stop the snowdrifts. We passed the grave of Kelso, the famous racehorse, across from the Cole farm on Route 301. My father pulled over near a stand of scrub pines and told me to get out of the car. He opened the trunk and leashed the dog, and she strained against the leather, her nose to the ground, her round, metal dog tags clinking brightly. Then he took a handgun from his coat pocket and shot the dog once in the head. I recall her open, brown eyes, the sound of a loud crack repeating in the frozen air, and a small spray of blood on the snow. Everything turned black and white and gray, and I rose up through the bare trees, higher and higher, until I saw everything from a great distance, and the crescent of pink tongue lying on the dog's thin black lips became so small I could not see it anymore. *Like time in a snow globe. The scenery is all pines and snowy fields when I turn the sphere. In the foreground is a child, poised in silence, waving goodbye or hello, we don't know. A balance of snow and light and sorrow hovers there.*

The animals in my poems have come to represent the part of me I had to shut down to survive the constant potential for violence that permeated the air I breathed as a girl. We ate the game my father brought home during various hunting seasons, the chest freezer packed full of meat wrapped in white paper and labeled with a magic marker. My father could dismember rabbits and then pull their fur coats off in one piece, leaving only their pink, sinewy flesh. When he "bagged" a buck, he cut off the antlers and boiled the hair from the skullcap in a pot on the kitchen stove. In the utility room, where he kept his tools, the antlers rested on a shelf above my mother's washing machine. And so my childhood and later my poems became filled with the ghosts of animals: Bell, nosing the snow for a rabbit's scent; the *dead deer trophy draped across the car's hood, the bloody bullet hole in the animal's side, a secret place I could crawl into and hide;* the *fox, its hide sunken around bleached-white, beautiful bones, lingering in new grass, warming the stones;* or the *fish, open-eyed, half-eaten* that *returned my startled gaze as it turned and turned in the trail of foam the boat's motor made.*

"Groundhogging with My Father" (1986), for example, is a lyrical account of one of the many slayings I witnessed. Mr. Carter, a local farmer, hired my father to rid his fields of groundhogs that were ravaging the tender soybean plant-shoots. My father instructed me to look through the powerful scope to view the animals in the crosshairs. I could see the black whiskers on the animal's face and its jaw muscles working rapidly to masticate the soybean leaves. Then he squeezed *the trigger with an expert, breathless motion, sending grasshoppers unhinged from the dust and the groundhog hurling backwards, its head filling with light.* I do not know if my father even thought about how witnessing the slaughter of animals might impact me, but

> . . . they still come back to me,
> blaze up in clear memory
> of our rides on rutted dirt roads,
> five dead groundhogs resting
> in the trunk of our car, blood blossoms
> thickening on bristly fur and flies
> humming in the heat: a melody measured
> occasionally now by the distant
> buzz in the frozen air of my neighbor's power
> saw, or the drone of a scholar reading obscure
> texts in the university library, murmuring
> his learned language as I walk by.
> I locate my childhood precisely at such moments
> and see myself at ten, studying the brooding
> groundhog shape as I listened

VANESSA HALEY

74

for danger at the field's flowering
boundary, where I stood among burdock
and took aim again and again
at the ineffable
while pollen swarmed in a golden haze,
and insects resumed their own diminishing.

After the shooting, my father would wind his way on the bumpy dirt road back to the farmer's house and report his killing numbers to Mrs. Carter, who had just gathered a wire-mesh basket of fresh eggs. Just that spring her only son had been crushed by the tractor he was driving when one wheel slipped into a ditch. His name was Robert, a sturdy boy with dark, curly hair and blue eyes. His eighth-grade school picture rested in a cardboard frame on the mantel above the large kitchen fireplace. Death was everywhere on a farm, and I suppose Mrs. Carter did not give it a second thought that a ten-year-old girl was watching her father shoot animals relegated to the "pest" category when the price of soybeans was dropping.

Mrs. Carter boxed a dozen brown eggs in a stained, gray carton and handed them to me. My father drove to the other side of town toward Silver Lake. We passed fields owned by the Green Giant company, where migrant workers—mostly Mexicans—crouched all day in the hot sun, picking tomatoes and loading bushel baskets onto flatbed trucks. When our car turned down the dirt lane leading up to the shacks that served as housing for the workers, three short, dark women waved and smiled as though they knew my father. He got out, walked to the back of the car, and opened the trunk, and then he and the women carried the groundhogs into one of the shacks. A whirligig of orange dust swirled up around the small procession, and a dog rushed forward from the dark hollow of an overturned oil drum, until it suddenly jerked backward when its chain came up short. It barked and lunged and half-choked itself until we drove away. I remember watching the dog in the side-view mirror until it vanished into the black hole of its home.

"What are they going to do with the groundhogs?" I asked. I opened the cardboard carton and examined the eggs. A hairline crack zigzagged across the top of one. My blonde hair was flying all around my head in the windy interior. When my father turned to me I saw myself duplicated in his reflector sunglasses.

"Don't fool with those eggs, goddamn it," he shouted. He sped the rest of the way home until he slammed on the brakes about a foot from our garage door, and I was catapulted into the dashboard. I knew better than to cry, even when my nose started to bleed. "Jesus Christ," he hissed. "You broke Mrs. Carter's eggs." My head was throbbing. In slow motion, it seemed, I reached for the car-door handle, and he squeezed my knee hard enough to bend me over. "Where do you think you are going?" he asked. "You think you're getting away?"

I had been trying to get away ever since then. Away from the claustrophobic house of my childhood, away from the small town bordered by four graveyards, away from the double negatives and enraged expletives I heard at home, away from the range of my father's rifle scopes, away from his reach; indeed, away from my own body: *We long to rise above the body we have always known, relishing the absence of weight, drifting past marsh lilies at the water's edge, inevitably drawn toward an abstraction called light.* I learned to vanish, *like fish fading back in dark water,* or like the snapping turtle my father decapitated in front of me: *for a long time in the sunlight it opened and closed its mouth, wordless, as though articulating the particulars of absence.*

My tendency to shut down and to internalize the trauma—to "dissociate" in psychological terms—served as both vehicle and obstacle to my healing and creativity. "Where are you?" Frances would ask, and I came back to the present, to her book-and-plant-filled office, to her kind, intelligent voice. As difficult as it was for me to disclose the details of the abuse, I realized it was a necessary part of the journey. No amount of cleaning, ordering, neatening, numbing, or blanking out could erase the past. More importantly, I wanted to feel comfortable in my own body.

According to poet Edward Hirsch, "Implicit in poetry is the notion that we are deepened by heartbreak, that we are not so much diminished as enlarged by grief, by our refusal to vanish—to let others vanish—without leaving a verbal record."[1] Here Hirsch is not simply repeating a cliché, that "what doesn't kill us makes us stronger." He is crediting those who attempt to leave a verbal record so that they or others will not vanish despite the heartbreak. For what is writing and reading poetry if not an honest attempt at sympathetic identification? And what is the purpose of psychotherapy if not to speak one's truth and to be heard and understood? If my poems are revised, honed-down, reorganized versions of my life's most salient moments, and testaments to my own refusal to disappear, then psychotherapy helped me gain the insight and emotional stamina to write.

After approximately sixty psychotherapy sessions—recognizing my post-traumatic stress symptoms and developing adaptive coping strategies to alleviate my anxiety and depression—I had to look directly at what had been lost to me and grieve what was gone. Lyric poetry became a parallel vehicle through which I could rebuild my lost self. I wrote fragments (stream-of-consciousness prose) describing both positive and negative memories and shared them with Frances, who listened and observed, "Now you are the author of your own life." Slowly, I was able to externalize my terror and recognize that, although my father's violence and cruelty had contributed heavily to my PTSD and obsessive-compulsive behaviors, I was now, as an adult, responsible for how I managed my own well-being.

Therapy helped me retrieve and connect to the displaced part of me I had stored away long ago in my efforts to block the fear and anxiety I experienced as a small child, but it also helped me stay grounded and feel safe enough to process those feelings. Louise DeSalvo describes the therapeutic resurrection of the lost self we engage in when we write about (and thereby impose our own order on) past events that were disturbing or chaotic: "Confronting the chaos of our most difficult memories and feelings, though, and translating them into coherent language can have 'remarkable short-and-long-term health benefits.' For when we deal with unassimilated events, when we tell our stories and describe our feelings and integrate them into our sense of self, we no longer must actively work at inhibition. This alleviates the stress of holding back our stories and repressing or hiding our emotions, and so our health improves."[2]

THE POINT IS NOT to allow the self to get erased. My sessions with Frances twenty years ago taught me that when I felt mildly dissociative, it was probably due to a subtle trigger in my environment that reminded me, unconsciously, of past trauma. Gradually, she gave me the skills necessary to reel myself in from the drift mode and remain anchored in the here and now. I learned what magical thinking was and that my preoccupation with the number four was something I could gradually relinquish as I reconditioned myself to reduce the frequency of my counting rituals. After I prepared a lecture I read it over only three, then two, then only one time before the class began. Instead of calculating my bus stop four blocks from campus, I got off the bus closer to the English department building. The emotional competency I gained in therapy enabled me to tap into details of past trauma, without feeling controlled by those events. I could integrate the past as something that had shaped me but did not define me. "Blackbird" (1998) perhaps best reflects such resiliency.

No one is home except me and my father,
who pushes with even strides the lawn mower
across the yard once a week. I can hear
the motor compete with cicadas vibrating near
my bedroom window. All summer they fly
to the maples, protest the inevitable. They lie
overturned: white undersides, wings intricate
as leaf veins or the labyrinth I construct
when the motor cuts off and I know
what comes next. The door opens.
I am already well ahead of him,
running through a dim maze, pressing
against panels, triggering escape hatches,
his whispers diminished by my own footsteps
echoing down a long pale corridor. It helps
afterward if I go outside on the fresh cut
grass and hunt for pieces left
behind: toads whose leap was seconds slow,
whose last thoughts were of the man's shadow,
their leathery limbs and golden heads
scattered. They didn't feel a thing. Instead
of looking for me when Mother returns from work,
she fixes him a glass of iced tea, ignores
my solitary games, my macabre fascination
with the dead. In a tone of elation,
a voice that saddens me still, she thanks him
for the beautiful lawn, for taking care of things.
Memory litters an otherwise perfect landscape, and I
realize the cloudless, sulphur-blue sky
promises me nothing,
not a star nor horizon. But something
in the moon's thin shell lets me bury there
my life's distorted picture, where
the brain empties the face of a girl,
her red-winged heart flying like a blackbird
through the other side of childhood.

This poem, more than any of my other work, illustrates DeSalvo's notion that, by imposing our own order on the chaos of trauma, we gain a sense of mastery in the creation of a new, restored self. Although the child becomes "scattered" like the toads run over by the lawn mower and is "overturned" like the vulnerable cicadas, she "constructs" a labyrinth filled with "escape hatches" and secret "panels." The adult (retrospective) narrator allows for the possibility of hope that the girl somehow survived "life's distorted picture," her spirit metamorphosed into the "red-winged heart flying like a blackbird through the other side of childhood." This is not to say that my poems are imbued with a Pollyannic vision as a result of therapy. The *work* I did with Frances was exactly that: an arduous, painful, but ultimately worthwhile endeavor that helped me realize that while *the cloudless, sulphur-blue sky promises me nothing, not a star nor horizon, . . . something in the moon's thin shell* gave me reason to believe that healing was possible. Psychotherapy and writing lyric poetry are still the vehicles I use to help me sort through the rough terrain of inevitable losses that accompany us in middle age and to assist me in my efforts to retrieve and restore the distant parts of me that sometimes detach and drift almost out of reach.

NOTES

1. Edward Hirsch, *How to Read a Poem: And Fall in Love with Poetry* (New York: Harcourt, Brace, 1999), 81.

2. Louise DeSalvo, *Writing as a Way of Healing: How Telling Our Stories Transforms Our Lives* (Boston: Beacon Press, 1999), 24–25.

Eight

THE USES OF DEPRESSION

THE WAY AROUND IS THROUGH

DAVID BUDBILL, MDiv

WHEN I WAS A TEENAGER, I was involved in music and theater. I played jazz trumpet pretty seriously and I was in a couple of high school plays. I didn't get interested in writing poetry until I was a senior. The deeper, the more intense my interest in writing poetry grew, the deeper and more intense my periods of depression became also. By the time I was half way through college I was writing a lot of poetry and spending a lot of time lying on a cot in a depressive and paralytic daze down in the dark of a basement furnace room. Clearly, or so it seemed to me, poetry and depression were lovers doing some kind of macabre dance in and with my life, and I was, it appeared, helpless, no matter how much I resisted, to do anything about it. This was in the late 1950s.

This pattern of bursts of creativity—making poems, stories, plays, essays—alternating with periods of paralytic depression was to be the way I lived my life for the next thirty years. I started calling "her" The Angel of Depression.

LETTER TO THE ANGEL OF DEPRESSION

O, Angel of depression, I give myself to you.
I give myself to you Angel of darkness, Angel
of quiet pain, Angel of numbness, Angel of a
stillness still as death, Angel of the eyes that stare,
Angel of the breath that barely moves, Angel of
dullness, I give myself to you. I give myself to you.
I praise you. I pay homage to you. I attend to you.
I do not turn my back on you. I make this prayer
for you. I speak it openly in front of everyone. O,

Angel of darkness, Angel of depression, dark Angel
of life, I do not forget you. Therefore, now,
I pray you, give me leave,
release me, let me go.

uncollected poem

But my ablutions didn't get me much absolution. For many years in my
twenties, thirties, and forties, it sometimes seemed that I was going to
lose this battle with depression. Sometimes I thought suicide was the
only way out.

I HAVE ALWAYS BEEN and still am a rebellious, contrary sort of person and writer, always going against the mainstream, no matter what
that mainstream is.

FLAWED VERSE: AFTER A POEM BY HAN SHAN

Vinegar Bob, The Academic, laughs at my flawed verse and says,
*He writes short stories, then chops up the lines so he can pretend
they're poems.*
  I say: What's wrong with short stories?

Vinegar Bob, The Academic, laughs at my flawed verse and says,
*He has no command of prosody. He just throws words down
anywhere on the page.*
  I say: Yeah, that's right. I'll throw 'em down anywhere I like.

from Moment to Moment: Poems of a Mountain Recluse

THIRTY-FIVE YEARS ALONE

Thirty years alone at the foot of Judevine Mountain raising
    vegetables, cutting
firewood, talking to the birds and making poems, hasn't exactly
made Judevine Mountain a household word in the poetry
    academy.

Once a friend recommended him to the academy and they all
    cried,
Who's this Judevine Mountain guy? Another friend—who just
happened to be there—said, *Everybody in these parts knows who
    he is.*

THE USES OF DEPRESSION

Why, he's the most famous unknown poet for miles around. The only people
around here who don't know who he is, is you! Which, of course, proved
to the academy that he didn't exist at all. And therefore

Judevine Mountain was set free to continue on his mountainside
raising vegetables, cutting firewood, talking to the birds and making poems,
which he is doing to this very day, in his non-existent sort of way.

from *While We've Still Got Feet*

In 1981, at the age of forty-one, I received a Guggenheim Fellowship in Poetry. The Establishment—with a capital T and a capital E—had opened its arms and welcomed me in. It was more than I could stand. Almost immediately I fell into a depression deeper and more profound than any I had ever experienced. I sat in a chair all day, day after day, and cried.

WHEN YOU WERE FOUR AND I WAS FORTY-ONE

for my daughter, Nadine

When you were four and I was forty-one
and sunk in my depression deeper than I'd ever been—
when all day each day all I could do was sit in a chair
and stare and weep at nothing in particular—
in the morning you'd come down the stairs still in
your pink sleeper and find me there already in my chair
or still there from the night before already staring
or weeping in that paralysis that was my life then,
you'd climb up into the chair and settle yourself,
fit yourself, curl yourself, into my lap so I could
hold you in my sadness while I wept and never,
not ever, not once, did you ask me why
I was crying, nor did you ever ask me to explain.

Now, twenty years later, now that you are twenty-four
and I am sixty-one I write this to say to you, Nadine,
you were such warmth, such sweet serenity,
such peace and comfort to me then. Thank You, Nadine,
My Daughter, for the chance to hold you when you were four
and I was forty-one.

uncollected poem

I was beginning to get an ulcer. My doctor put me on the Sippy Diet—only bland foods, no booze, no tomatoes, no spicy food of any kind. In other words, none of the foods I loved the most. No red wine, pasta, and red sauce. My god! forbidden to eat the most calming, relaxing, soporific meal known to humanity! I got worse—fast.

Next my doctor prescribed Ativan, but, because I'm hypersensitive to all drugs, my reaction to it was horrific. I felt so detached from myself I thought I had died. Over and over again, I had a vision of myself standing inside a telephone booth looking outside at myself while the self outside jumped up and down waving his arms and screaming at the top of his lungs, but the self inside the telephone booth just stood there motionless—and *emotion*less—staring at the self outside. All the self inside the booth could hear was a slight wind blowing. I was scared to death. It was as if the drug had split me in two: there was still a real self full of emotion out there jumping around waving his arms, but he was unapproachable, unreachable. The self I knew was a zombie. How was I going to create anything in this condition?

Then one night, while I was on the road for a reading in Buffalo, New York, I lay awake all night, my heart racing, beating maybe two hundred fifty beats a minute, maybe more. I don't know why. Perhaps it was a side effect of Ativan.

The next morning my heart rate had returned, somehow, to something like normal. I swore that morning never to take another tablet of Ativan or any other psychotropic drug again. I never have. It was clear to me that I'd have to deal with this problem without pharmaceuticals.

OVER THE ALMOST twenty-five years since then I've developed my own way of dealing with and using my depression. And as I've grown older, my periods of depression have lessened in both duration and intensity. I don't know why.

I've developed for myself what I call the "give in" method. I've discovered that the only way around my periods of depression is directly through them; in other words, the sooner I can resign myself to the Angel of Depression, the sooner she will be done with me and leave me alone. I should note here that I've been able to resign myself to her when necessary because I've been a free-lance writer for the past more than thirty-five years and therefore I don't have a nine-to-five job. I do have to travel quite a bit, and the Angel seems to be kind enough to let me have those trips out and not bother me. This is an agreement we've come to later in my life. When I was younger she took me over whenever and wherever she wanted, with no consideration for what I had to do. In short, the quicker I can let the Angel of Depression take over my life completely and have her way with me for as long as she needs to, the sooner I can get back to my life.

WHEN I GET DEPRESSED

I get silent and I stare
    at nothing all day long,
or I lie down and read
    the ancient masters who
move me to even greater
    depths of melancholy,

and then,
    refreshed,

I get up
    and
join the world
    again.

from *Moment to Moment: Poems of a Mountain Recluse*

My depressions come most predictably near or just after the equinoxes.

THE END OF WINTER

The delicate and lovely emptiness of winter
    gone now today, suddenly gone,
        this last week
        of May.

The glut of summer rushed in,
    grass crowding everything,
        trees thick again
        with green.

The whole world full of life and noise
    closing in, and nowhere for us
        dark ones, depressed ones
        to hide.

from *Moment to Moment: Poems of a Mountain Recluse*

DAVID BUDBILL

Yellow leaves
    pile up
on the Scholar's
    ink stone.
His brush
    is dry.

He lies
    still as death
on his cot
    curled in
upon
    himself.

Gone away
    on his
autumnal
    wander
through
    Depression.

from While We've Still Got Feet

But, as I've said, as I've grown older both the duration and the intensity of these periods of depression have lessened. However, I want to try to explain why I think these periods of depression are actually good and useful and important to my writing life and to my life in general.

I WANT TO TALK about the Writer as Receptacle and then about Imagination Time in order to talk about Depression as Emptiness, all of which are a way of talking about The Uses of Depression.

THE WRITER AS RECEPTACLE

I have a little sign on my wall that says: "Don't think. Listen. Watch." When I apply my mind to the task at hand I can't hear what is there to be heard. In other words, if I think, I can't listen; when I use my head, my ears fall off.

I understand myself as a writer as someone who is a receiver, a receptacle. After I am filled up, or while I am being filled up, I can then attempt to become a transmitter of what I have received. I listen for the voices, and if I'm lucky I hear them and I write them down.

I'm a recordist, a stenographer, a secretary. If you want to get fancy about it, you could call me an intermediary, a priest. I don't invent what I write, I don't think it up, I record what I hear and see, both outside of me in the world and inside of me in my imagination, and most often in that combination of the two in which what is outside of me gets transformed into something new as it passes into the inside of me.

I do all this with language, which is not an end in itself, but a means to an end, the end of getting down on paper what I have received. My responsibility is to get down clearly and articulately what I have heard. Only as my capacity to be accepting and receiving comes together with my articulate use of the language is good work produced. If I haven't been articulate enough with the language, if my technique isn't good enough—well, too bad for me; I have failed. All of which is to say, I am responsible *only* for my mediocre and bad work. I can't take credit for my good work, since I am only the conduit for it. This notion has a pleasant sense of humility about it which appeals to me.

I want to dwell for a moment on the passive, accepting, receiving aspect of being a writer. This may be an issue particularly for men, since to be open, passive, receptive, and fecund is not the way most boys are raised; but increasingly it is an issue for women writers, too, inasmuch as we live in an age that gives so much credence and value to aggressiveness, assertiveness, and to the positive, optimistic, light, active, "male," Yang virtues. At the same time, our age denigrates the "female," Yin virtues of darkness, passivity, receptiveness, and so on. I understand that the idea of the Yielding Female—whether applied to men or women—is not currently a popular idea.

All that notwithstanding, here are a few excerpts pertaining to the idea of the Yielding Female, to the dark, passive, receptive, unknowing Yin virtues, from *The Tao Te Ching*. (These translations are my own compilations and inventions based on translations by Robert Payne, Witter Bynner, Gia-Fu Feng, and Jane English.)

Chapter 6 of *The Tao Te Ching* says:

> The dark valley spring never dies.
> It is called the Mysterious Female.
> The entrance to the Mysterious Female
> is the root of Heaven and Earth.
> The entrance is quiet and hidden, seldom seen.
> Touch it. Use it. It will never fail, never run dry.

DAVID BUDBILL

Chapter 10 says:

> At the entrance to the Mysterious Female
> Can you take the part of the woman?
> All seeing, all knowing, open to everything
> Can you lie back and do nothing?

Chapter 20 says:

> All men are beaming with pleasure
>
> . . . .
> I alone am silent. I am a simpleton,
> a do-nothing. I am like an infant.
> Abandoned, like someone homeless.
> Men of the world are rich and successful,
> They have position, power, prestige.
> I alone seem to have nothing.
> I am a man with the mind of an idiot.
> A pure fool. I am dull and stupid.
> Everywhere men are so clever and witty,
> They are always so self-confident.
> I never know what I'm doing.
> I alone am dark and disquieted.
> I am restless as a nervous sea,
> All I ever do is drift. I never get anywhere.
> Everywhere men are making their mark on the world
> While I am depressed and sad,
> aimless and full of regret.
> I am different from all these others!
> All I want to do is lie with the Mysterious Female.
> All I want to do is suck at the mother's breast.

Chapter 28 says:

> Know the male, but cleave to the female.
> Know the light, but love the dark
> Thus you will become the root of heaven and earth,
> the womb of the world, and you will give birth
> continuously, endlessly.

But how do you conceive? What is the proper atmosphere for fertile conception?

I need—I think we all do—the one thing it seems is the most difficult to get in our lives: time. Very few of us can knock out poems in every
little spare moment or two the way William Carlos Williams did between patients in his doctor's office. We need time to empty ourselves
out so that we can be filled up again. We need time for emptiness, not
for business, for busy-ness.

This kind of emptiness, sloth, laziness, is absolutely un-American.
It runs contrary to the hurrying, consumptive, thingy, acquisitive,
thoughtless American way. We are all busy, so busy busy busy, and we
are proud of being busy. In fact, if you aren't so busy you are about to
go nuts, you really aren't successful, and everybody knows it. Besides,
being busy means you are the one in charge.

THE BUSY MAN SPEAKS

Appointments, schedules, deadlines.
Demands on my time from everywhere.
I've got to plan every minute.

I'm so busy and important I don't have time to
trust the current like an unmoored boat.

I wouldn't want to anyway.
I make the current go
where *I* want it to go.
I'm in charge here.

from *While We've Still Got Feet*

Trust the current like an unmoored boat—in other words, just drift
along—is a quote from the ancient Chinese poet, Han Shan, one of the
great do-nothing guys of all time, the exact opposite of an in-charge
kind of guy. In fact, I'd say, bluntly, if you need to be in charge, you
can't be a poet.

SUCH SELF-INDULGENCE AND SLOTH!

All morning I sit at my desk drinking tea,
reading ancient poets
and writing my own ridiculous poems.

DAVID BUDBILL

In the afternoon I go wandering through the woods
to see wildflowers and listen to birds
and the wind singing through the trees.

Then I sit beside the brook down in the bottom
of the ravine where the rock outcroppings loom
over my head, and I listen to the waterfall.

Such self-indulgence and sloth makes me so happy!
I wonder who will pay me to be useless and in love?

from *Moment to Moment: Poems of a Mountain Recluse*

We have to be—I have to be, at least—empty, open, quiet, passive, receptive, dark. I have to do nothing in order to be filled.

This kind of emptiness is akin to the Zen Buddhist concept of Emptiness or what, in Zen art, would be called "negative space," all that blank paper surrounding the little ink painting of the bowl down in the lower right-hand corner, all that silence in and around much shakuhachi music, all that incredibly slow slow slow Butoh dancing.

WHERE I LIVE

Where I live is
        emptiness.

Time to watch
        and listen.

Space between
        events and people.

Room for thoughts
        to wander.

There they go—
        drifting

wherever
        they want to.

I've got no discipline at all!

from *Moment to Moment: Poems of a Mountain Recluse*

THE USES OF DEPRESSION

In my life at least, depression is a kind of emptiness, a slothful, no-thing, withdrawal from the world. Although I've said that giving in to these periods of depression is the quickest way through them, I want to also say that over the years I've discovered that these periods of depression are not entirely negative. There is a positive aspect to depression.

I've come to understand my periods of depression not as useless periods in my life, periods that are to be fought against and resisted, but as dormancy periods, gestation periods, to be accepted, given in to, welcomed.

Over the years many very interesting and useful notes, images, situations, phrases, and so forth have appeared to me, have come to me—I've heard them—during these periods of depression. But more often I have no idea what is going on during the period of depression. Only much later do I realize that, because of that period of emptiness, I am now full of something new.

Botanists know that trees require their period of dormancy in the winter in order to grow during the summer. It appears that trees, while dormant, aren't really asleep, but rather are storing up energy for the coming burst of growth. No periods of growth without also periods of rest. Could this be one of the functions of depression?

Another great and useful use of depression is that it keeps you in touch with an acute sense of failure—not that most of us most of the time need any reminding of what it is like to fail. This contact with a sense of failure is especially necessary for anyone who is lucky enough to become even modestly successful. Not only does it keep you in touch with your real self, the self you know in the privacy of your own despair, but it also keeps you in touch with the depths of common humanity. This intense sense of failure, especially at the times of success, creates wholeness. It's a wholesome and honest blend of light and dark.

The Yin/Yang symbol is a circle evenly divided into half dark and half light, but the halves are not opposing; they are wrapped around each other. The line between them is not a straight line but a French curve; the dark and the light embrace each other; they are inseparably entwined, as in the number 69. Furthermore, within the dark space there is a nucleus of light, and within the light space a nucleus of dark.

The back and forth in my own life between periods of active writing and passive, do-nothing periods of depression seem to keep me going. I can't have one without the other. And now, as I grow older—I'm sixty-seven—my periods of depression are fewer and fewer and their intensity less and less. Maybe I'm not so compulsive or ambitious anymore. I don't worry so much about my periods of not writing. I actually enjoy them. I work in my gardens, cut wood, play my shakuhachi, do nothing. In other words, I wait.

A CAVE ON JUDEVINE MOUNTAIN

There is a cave on Judevine Mountain, a secret place,
way back in the woods, high up on a hidden slope,

in a place no one ever goes. Only I know where it is.
No one else has ever been there. I go up there a lot

and sit around, make a little fire, boil some tea,
sometimes cook a little meal, but mostly what I do is

sit and wait, poke at the fire, add a twig or two
and wait and wait and stare, until suddenly

I know what to do.

from *While We've Still Got Feet*

And sometimes what I suddenly know what to do is more of nothing.

Which brings me to wonder about the function of psychotropic drugs and whether in some cases they actually hinder a creative person from getting in touch with his or her dark, depressive side, actually get in the way of that dormancy some call depression, which may actually be a period of important creative gestation for what comes next.

Nine

IN THE MIDDLE OF LIFE'S JOURNEY

JACK COULEHAN, MD

In the middle of the journey of our life
I found myself astray in a dark wood
where the straight road had been lost sight of.

WHEN, AS A YOUNG MAN, I first read the opening stanza of Dante's *Inferno*, I probably raced right passed it without thought because I was so anxious to delve into the nitty-gritty of hell. However, when I took up Dante again in the mid-1980s, the same three lines jumped up and hooked me. Dante's experience hit home. At the time I found myself in Pittsburgh following a variety of roads that seemed irreconcilable. I was a primary care internist in an academic medical center, an epidemiologist studying cardiovascular disease in Navajo Indians, and a nascent student of doctor-patient communication. I had plenty of energy. It was exhilarating to jump from crunching numbers to talking with patients to making rounds in the hospital. Yet something was missing, not only a piece of the puzzle, but *the* piece that I yearned for. I felt very much "astray in a dark wood."

In this essay I reflect upon the effects of psychiatric treatment on my creative writing, especially poetry. Before I can do so, however, I need to explain that when I found myself in the dark wood, I was not writing poetry and hadn't been for at least twelve years. I believe psychotherapy allowed me to seize an unexpected opportunity that arose when a patient offered to become my poetry teacher. This led to my becoming a writer, which I think saved my life. For me, poetry was the path I was looking for. Much later, during another spell of psychiatric treatment, I began to take medication that had an additional influence on my life and work, as both a poet and a physician. Thus, this story has three parts: a prepsychotherapeutic prelude; psychotherapy, followed by a long span of poetic development and synergism between medical practice and poetry; and, finally, the addition of antidepressant medication and its effects on my writing.

Ever since I sent maudlin poems to my girlfriends in high school, I fancied myself a creative writer. At St. Vincent, a Benedictine college known best for its proximity to the home of Rolling Rock beer, I wrote a poem for a freshman English assignment. It was an elegant pseudo-Eliot affair with internal rhymes and classical references. Father Maynard called me into his office after class and told me in no uncertain terms that I was a plagiarist. "You picked the wrong teacher to mess with," he said, with the tone of a hawk descending on its rabbit. "There's no way you could have written a poem like this."

"I did, Father," I sheepishly told the crucifix behind his left ear. "Really."

Benedictines were very existential in those days, and Maynard was one of the most exceptionally existential of the lot. I wrote him poem after poem filled with angst and *being-for* and references to Sartre. Because of this, he took me aside and suggested that I major in English and concentrate on writing. But I turned him down. "Biology," I said. "I want to help people. I want to be a doctor. But I can still write, can't I?"

I completed college totally naive about the medical life; never volunteered in a hospital or nursing home or even had a local physician role model. When growing up, I was rarely sick. When a cold or sore throat did develop, my mother's prescription was inevitably aspirin and juice. On occasion I did venture into old Doc McGee's office. He lived in a huge yellow house near our church and intimidated me because he was a parish big shot and a cigar smoker as well. In addition, his smart-ass son was my nemesis. Given this record of naiveté and noninvolvement, a medical school admissions committee today would never even grant me an interview, but things were different in 1965.

So why choose medicine? My role model was Albert Schweitzer, who at that time was the Great Humanitarian of the World. He appealed to me as a Renaissance man—philosopher, theologian, musicologist, musician, physician, and missionary. As a teenager in southwestern Pennsylvania, I visualized myself at Schweitzer's side treating elephantiasis in the jungles of Gabon and, in the evening, listening to him play Bach chorales under the African sky. I remember reading (with little understanding) his early masterpiece, *The Quest for the Historical Jesus*, and struggling with his concept of "reverence for life" in *Civilization and Ethics*. Here was a man who ranged from the world of abstract ideas to that of human suffering, from the security of church and university to the riskiness of Central Africa. What intensity! What romance! Thus, I became convinced that medicine was for me—but on semi-Schweitzerian terms, which in my case would include becoming a famous poet as well as a beloved healer and humanitarian.

Fast forward about fifteen years. After completing a residency in internal medicine and a master's degree in public health, I spent two years practicing on a Navajo reservation in Arizona and then solidified into a faculty position at the University of Pittsburgh medical school. My Schweitzerian dreams had grown (or perhaps diminished) into a variety of practical tasks and responsibilities, but one aspect had atrophied almost completely. By the time I reached my mid-forties, I was a confirmed imaginary poet. That is, I imagined myself to be a poet— convinced that wisdom and beauty were poised to burst forth from my pen at any moment, if only I had the time to write, which I didn't. It was a vicious cycle. While I still considered "poet" as part of my identity, I was "forced" to stifle my brilliance because medical practice, teaching, research, and family life made too many demands. While my family and profession provided many emotional rewards, something was missing. I gravitated toward studying the physician-patient relationship, while becoming less and less interested in the dramatic world of medical technology. I began to write about empathy, ethics, and communication, an array of topics relatively new to medicine in the early 1980s. Nonetheless, I felt keenly locked in and helpless to break out, which made me angry. I blamed myself, but more consciously I blamed my boss, the medical school, and everything else that was standing in my way. Anger led to depression, which, in turn, aggravated my helplessness.

POETRY AS THERAPY

I can't remember the precipitating factor that led me to seek psychotherapy. Whatever it was, it broke down my strong defense against asking for help. Even though I had become something of an expert in treating primary care patients with anxiety and depression, and typically explained to them in detail that these were true medical problems, not manifestations of weakness or failure, I never thought that particular spiel applied to me. To admit that my life was getting out of control had been unthinkable until then. My chief complaint was oppression related to work: "I'm hemmed in." "I feel like I'm trapped." "If only I had time to write." My goal was to get off my butt so I could look for a new job. But what job? Although functioning productively in day-to-day work, whenever I tried to plan for the future, I couldn't get past the stage of vague Schweitzerian dreams.

My psychiatrist was Central European and analytically trained, almost the stereotype of an old-time talking psychiatrist, whose office was in a house on a leafy street several blocks from the hospital. A metaphor that appeared frequently in our sessions was the huge boulder that I carried on my back, an enormous weight at the nape of my neck that pressed me to the ground. I staggered under the load, so much so I couldn't progress in any one direction but had to step this way and that to balance the weight. Otherwise, I'd lose control and the boulder would crush the people around me. Later in our conversations, the boulder turned into a tangled web of uncertainties that held me back, like wild rose or kudzu. I was lost in thorns, unable to make a serious effort at becoming a creative writer because of fear of failure.

"Or maybe you're just afraid to succeed," he said.

Afraid to succeed? What, *me* afraid to succeed? His comment struck home. It suddenly reframed my pattern of drawing back physically and emotionally and not rocking the boat. In fact, I had withdrawn to my cabin in the boat, rather than standing up and steering it. "Maybe you're just afraid to succeed"—twenty years later, this is the only specific interchange I remember from our sixteen or eighteen sessions, which dribbled off rather undramatically. I had learned not to feel ashamed about seeing a psychiatrist, but there seemed no resolution to my problems, not even a concrete step forward. I was anxious to please, though, and when he said we were coming to the end of our time together, I had to agree. Okay, I said to myself, you're feeling better. You must be. And then, during the last phase of therapy, a breakthrough *did* occur, although it came from an unexpected direction.

I had a patient named Rosaly Roffman, a poet and professor of English at a nearby state university. A mutual friend, who knew my poetic ambitions, had referred her for a chronic medical problem. Each time Rosaly came to my office, she made a point of asking to see my old poetry. When a patient tries to make friends like this, the proper professional response is to set clear limits. "This is about you, Rosaly; it's not about me," I explained. I repeatedly declined her offer to read and critique the poems, partly because I was ashamed of them, but mostly because the concept seemed thoroughly unprofessional. Nonetheless, it was tempting. Here she was, a real poetry teacher. Wouldn't this be a great chance to discover if I had talent?

After a few months of hemming and hawing, I took the risk and gave her a stack of poems to read, most of them dating from college or medical school. In a week or so we arranged a meeting at the hospital snack bar to discuss them. All I remember about that meeting was being delighted by her enthusiasm. At the time I thought she was praising the quality of the work at hand, when, in fact, she was responding to her intuition of potential, not its achievement.

This was the beginning of a mentoring relationship that lasted several years. Rosaly and I developed a quid pro quo arrangement in which I provided free medical care ("professional courtesy") in exchange for her services as a teacher. She gave me assignments—for example, *Write a poem about the brother you never had*—and we would meet periodically to critique the work. These were extremely painful sessions. How dare she trash my wonderful lines! Doesn't she realize how good this is? I'm not going to subject myself to this abuse again! But the discipline and pain released a flood of creative energy. The stuff really *was* bad, but her gentle prodding drove me to make it better. Under Rosaly's tutelage I became a working poet.

Many of the early poems gave voice to aspects of patient care that I had felt since medical school but couldn't articulate. For example, "The Knitted Glove" expresses my intense frustration with the frequent situations in which I couldn't put my finger on, or even name, the source of a patient's suffering:

> This thing, the name for your solitary days,
> for the hips, the hand, for the walk of your eyes
> away from mine, this thing is coyote, the trickster.
> I want to call, Come out, you son of a dog!
> and wrestle that thing to the ground for you,
> I want to take its neck between my hands.
> But in this world I don't know how to find
> the bastard, so we sit. We talk about the pain.

Other poems gave voice to patients. Interestingly, these personae usually expressed anger or dissatisfaction with the way they were being treated by physicians. In "I'm gonna slap those doctors," a middle-aged man who used a wheelchair after polio cries out against the surgeons who inappropriately treated him for alcohol withdrawal because, given his gruffness and loud mouth, they wrongly assumed he was a heavy drinker. He imagines giving the arrogant bastards a good slap:

> . . . They'll be spinning around
> drunk as skunks, heads screwed on backwards,
> and then Doctor Big Nose is gonna smell
> their breaths, wrinkle his forehead, and spin
> down the hall in his wheelchair
> on the way to the goddamn heavenly choir.

The dynamic was complex. Although based on real patients, these personae came from within me. Their voices expressed anger at doctors, disapprobation that was to some extent directed at myself. So my poetic windows looking out toward the world as experienced by patients (the detached and unfeeling behavior of many contemporary doctors) were at the same time windows looking into my interior world (feelings of anger and disappointment with myself).

As time went on, I began to write poems that took a step beyond the understandable aspects of patient care toward a more irrational dimension, where my experience with patients triggered epiphany or transformation; for example, the recollection of a recently deceased six-hundred-pound man who had occupied two beds in the intensive care unit:

> and this worthless and alien body,
> this six hundred pound man,
> I discover him beautiful.

In these works I tried to express my occasional breakthrough to an experience of reality in which everything is connected and interdependent. This experience was again like a window, but this time wide open—anxieties and hangups poured out, while the grace of healing poured in. I felt that the discipline of writing poems did not in itself carry me closer to internal harmony, but rather made me sufficiently alert and receptive, so that when a window appeared (apparently at random), I was able to soak up the harmony that passed through it.

Whether I applied this metaphor only to relationships with patients or to my life as a whole, most of the time was still windowless, although the walls of the room sometimes glowed with residual light. I began to experience more keenly the paradox in medicine of being simultaneously detached and connected. Hard and soft. Steady and tender. One instance was an event that occurred in 1990 during a visit to the Ogallala Sioux Reservation at Pine Ridge, South Dakota. I was invited to observe a Sun Dance, held near the site of the Massacre at Wounded Knee, when the Seventh US cavalry shot and killed about two hundred virtually defenseless Sioux men, women, and children. In the Sun Dance, men (and now women) seek to restore harmony to their broken lives by communing with their totemic spirits. During the dance a general healing ceremony takes place, in which dancers and medicine men invite spectators to pick up small stones and to form a great circle on the open field. They then dance slowly around the circle, stopping to bless each supplicant. I was moved to tears. Back in Pittsburgh, I put my stone in a little buckskin pouch that I carried with me in my briefcase or pocket. Later, I tried to evoke the unity of opposites (detachment-connection, material-spiritual, hard-soft) symbolized by the "Medicine Stone":

> This stone is an aspect of soul that lasts.
> This stone is a remnant of no account
> . . . .
> This stone is an aspect of soul that lasts.
> I call it my friend, my black stone friend.

Another stream of early poems constituted an attempt to recreate myself by changing my heritage, especially by creating a new father. I considered my real father too ordinary, too prosaic and weak; in fact, too much like me. At some level I also entertained an Adopted Child Fantasy because it seemed impossible that the vividness and passion that I had begun to experience could stem from his plodding weaknesses. My father was an Artist at heart, but the slings and arrows of hard economic times, war, and the misfortune of being the youngest son in a large dysfunctional Irish family had led him to abandon his calling and become a window dresser for women's wear stores and later a retail advertising manager. Why did he compromise? And, given his compromise, why hadn't he been more financially successful?

My response was a long series of poems, each one imagining the persona of a different father. Usually these figures were based on men with significant influence, either positive or negative, in my life. Their commonality was determination and strength of character, although the personality itself might be questionable, or even ugly. For example, "My Father Sends Me Out for Tobacco" reimagines my high school basketball coach:

My father, the Lebanese coach,
sends me out for tobacco
while the other guys take gym
. . . .
The players know
my father's rage will strike them
sometimes without warning,
throw them against their lockers
and hit unjustly where it hurts.

However, most of the father poems sketched more morally inspiring figures. Eventually, though, the healing power of language took over, and I found myself writing honestly about my real father and the rift between us disappearing. It was a rift I had never openly acknowledged, except in poems; my encounters with these poetic personae allowed me to understand myself and our relationship better, so I was able eventually to embrace him just as he was, with all his (and my) many defects:

                              . . . I waited too long
to redeem the war we carried on,
father and son, for fifty years. Well,
closeness, touching, matter now, not anger.
I'll make up your stories later.

I developed a passion for the life and work of Anton Chekhov, who came along in the mid-1990s to finally and definitively put Albert Schweitzer to rest. Chekhov's cool eye and warm heart made him a model, both for the elusive "key" I sought to the connection between doctor and patient and for a style of writing that remains cool and declamatory on the surface but glows with inner warmth. Unlike many physician-writers, Chekhov never turned away from his medical identity; in fact, he embraced it as central to his way of looking at, and writing about, the world. I eventually wrote fifty or sixty poems about Chekhov and the physician characters in his stories and plays, trying consciously to model his characteristic style of compassionate acceptance, as in *The Cherry Orchard:*

A miniature flower
thrives in the moisture
and dust of a broken

pavement—this is the gist
of the matter. We want
so strongly to believe
the flower will spread
everywhere. How quickly
it dies! If the disease
had a cure, we would not need
so many remedies.

As the 1990s progressed, my work evolved in many ways. One was the growth of irony, which made the poems richer but also harder and less immediate. I began to write on a broader range of topics, less frequently about medical situations. I viewed myself as striving for simplicity, yet my voice bucked and resisted—what felt simple in my head came to the page as complex. Meanwhile, I reexperienced going astray in the dark wood time and again, although with more mature resources to confront the situation. Finally, I sought psychiatric help. Thus began my personal relationship with antidepressant medications, specifically, serotonin reuptake inhibitors (SSRIs).

MEDICATION AND POETRY

As a general internist, I had for many years treated depressed patients and was quite comfortable with prescribing SSRIs and monitoring their effects. In fact, I had participated in a substantial research program regarding the recognition and treatment of major depression in primary care settings. Thus, I felt fairly sophisticated in knowing the outward aspects of antidepressive medications, but I had no idea what the internal experience was like. I had read Peter Kramer's *Listening to Prozac* and was generally aware of the controversy surrounding his claims. Moreover, I knew that indications for SSRIs had expanded as these drugs proved to be effective in ameliorating a variety of problems, such as chronic anxiety and obsessive-compulsive disorder. Yet, I thought of these medications as purely back-to-baseline treatment. Most depressed patients became less depressed. Their symptoms gradually resolved. At some point, many of them became symptom-free. As recommended, I encouraged these patients to continue taking their SSRI for a year or more, or even indefinitely, depending on their prior history of depression. Many were grateful that they felt better, but I don't recall anyone ever saying, "Wow, the Prozac has changed my life!" or, "Life is more vivid than ever before!" Maybe it happened but I just wasn't listening well enough.

When faced with the prospect of taking an SSRI myself, I approached it as an experiment. My cup of anxiety was overflowing; feelings of self-doubt and helplessness were nearly overwhelming. The placebo effect of trying something new, especially a treatment I believed in, was bound to be great. My greatest fear, however, was that taking the drug would diminish creativity. In retrospect, this fear was ridiculous; I had written very little poetry in the preceding six months, even though I conscientiously plodded away at it, being a strong believer in the 10 percent inspiration–90 percent perspiration point of view. Nevertheless, taking a psychiatric medication felt risky—after all, I had survived for fifty-eight years without artificially bumping up the serotonin in my brain. Yet, riskiness was also attractive.

I wasn't prepared for the effects. I had expected to feel less depressed and anxious, but not that my baseline life experience would change. I had never realized how much the interplay of chronic anxiety and obsessiveness framed my everyday affairs: the lack of assertiveness; an inability to say no to requests for extra work; a compulsion to complete every task in a timely and orderly way, without prioritizing; and a penchant for doggedly hanging on to old obligations, often self-imposed in the first place, when they had become unnecessary or even inordinately burdensome. These characteristics formed part of the personality matrix that I considered unchangeable. With paroxetine on board, the world appeared more vivid, but less threatening. My anxiety melted away, as if I were continuously on vacation. The obsessive traits softened, so I felt free to approach life in a more flexible manner. Despite this new experience of freedom, my productivity did not suffer; in fact, it increased.

The other surprising feature was that I didn't experience myself as different—that is, my feelings were different, but the "I" that had those feelings was the same Jack that had always been there, only richer in texture and more authentic. In many ways this was analogous to my early response to writing poetry, shortly after psychotherapy—I started to speak more strongly, but the voice had always been there.

The changes in my writing mostly emerged from existing "text" rather than being revolutionary. Strangely, one of these was a movement toward formal verse. Although I had previously fooled around with an occasional sonnet or sestina, in my first year on paroxetine I started to experiment with a wide variety of traditional forms, including villanelles, ballades, rondeaux, and pantoums, in addition to sonnets. Moreover, in my "normal" poems I began to use rhyme and regular stanza patterns more frequently.

To give an example: The pantoum is a devilishly difficult form that comes from Southeast Asia (Malaya) via the French. It consists of a series of quatrains in which the second and fourth lines of one quatrain become the first and third lines of the next; this pattern continues relentlessly until the poem comes full circle in the last quatrain, in which the second and fourth lines echo the first and third lines of the opening quatrain. Not only does this sound confusing, it also seems to guarantee superficiality. How can you say anything meaningful, given such a narrow and rigid framework? Here is part of "Deep Structures," a pantoum about memory, soul, and the brain's deep nuclei:

> I never knew how deep the structures were
> or why the words for them compelled my brain.
> Amygdaloid—the sound tripped off my tongue.
> And hippocampal gyrus made me sing.
>
> The rhythm of these words compels my brain
> The tendons in my hand have been eclipsed,
> but hippocampal gyrus makes me sing.
> For thirty years, still dancing from my tongue
>
> . . . .
>
> Amygdaloid is almost perfect self.
> And even though I judged my soul was lost,
> those deep archaic structures never budged.
> They form the links by which our lives connect.
>
> And even though I judged my soul was lost
> I never knew how deep its structures were,
> the links they make by which our lives connect.
> Amygdaloid! It dances from my tongue.

These are the first, second, sixth, and seventh stanzas of the twenty-eight-line poem. The idea was to recreate in words the rhythmic firing and complexity of neural networks, attempting to evoke mystery while at the same time seemingly denying the mystery.

My adoption of form was counterintuitive because the medication to a large extent freed me from obsessive tendencies. I don't know whether my need for order and compulsion to stick with behaviors that are nonproductive, even damaging, is a defense mechanism against chronic anxiety, or whether my anxiety occurs when I deviate from obsessive behaviors. Either way, paroxetine dissolved the hard edges of that personality "structure," leaving a more flexible version that I readily identified as self; somewhat like an effective weed killer that leaves the grass unharmed. But how, then, to explain my adoption of rigid form? I can't, except to say that I'm generally freer to experiment in many areas of life since taking the SSRI. In poetry I've tried to use form to enhance meaning (as in "Deep Structures"), but I have also felt comfortable changing or abandoning rules when they didn't work.

A second change I noticed was that humor crept into my work. When I look at my poems from the 1980s, with all their fierce images and compassionate tropes, the humorlessness is striking. They're in dead earnest. During the 1990s my use of irony blossomed and with it came spurts of bitter humor. More recently, the humor has become gentler; the poems in which it occurs, more playful and often self-deprecating, as in "Phrenology," a villanelle about love and baldness:

> Concavities and lumps above my ear
> speak narratives I never would have known
> before relentless loss of all my hair
>
> . . . .
>
> It shines with gratitude—I love your care
> for this old scalp, though never have I won
> a way to read the bumps above *your* ear,
> which even now are swathed in silver hair.

Finally, my explorations of the doctor-patient relationship are also freer, and some of them rather dark and subversive. I've commented on the epiphany, or "Eureka!," poems, which are open-ended, suggestive, and generally affirmative. Recently, I've dealt with the same material in what might be called "negative epiphanies." These poems evoke transformative experiences that are knotty and threatening to social order. To illustrate, I'll quote from "My Machine," a poem written some years before taking paroxetine but illustrative of the Dark Side that has recently taken a more prominent place beside the Light. The poem considers the implications of a machine that creates greater closeness between patient and doctor:

> If I had a machine to use
> in a case like yours
>
> . . . .
>
> I'd throw off the sham

of working in a reasoned way
to find the answers to your pain.
I'd use words from an archaic
neural poem and feel the pull

of healing, skin to skin, instead of
being neither man nor woman
and doing the decent thing. The ache
would be a price worth paying.

Life is Dante's dark wood. Twenty years after my first experience with psychiatric treatment, to which I attribute the beginning of my life as a poet, I've learned that there is no "straight path" to lose sight of. The paths branch; moral life is like a maze. Nonetheless, it is possible to move generally in a given direction. One can follow a personal compass to avoid going astray. In many ways, my life has been two steps forward and one step back, but I feel less astray now than I did when I first walked up the steps to that psychotherapist's office or when I shared those juvenile poems with my poetry teacher. The text continues to change. I'll conclude with the last few lines from a poem called "Identity," completed just recently:

. . . the way I feel today,
so vividly myself, so *grounded*,
you might say the first draft is done.
I'm in the process of revision.

Ten

BASIC HEART

DEPRESSION AND THE ORDINARY

RENÉE ASHLEY, MA

BASIC HEART

What can we do once we are ordinary?

—LYNNE SHARON SCHWARTZ

Sorrow has a horizontal habit; some souls' feet are bound.
Still the black bag of night is the structure of hope. Tonight's
Concert of blue light is riddled with the infinite; your jester's
Stripped of bells—neither fool nor the absolute fire behind
That black gate. The trees read the air and, despite the meticulous
Script of your bones, you sing your savage door wide and wear
The heart, finally, as just a heart, poor vessel of all your moments.

WRITING IS AN ACT of finding out what I know, and this is what
I know now: depression *for me* is what is ordinary. I face some aspect of
it every day. Even when the prescription drugs are working at their
best, I understand the possibilities of their failure. Experience has
taught me that somewhere, over my left shoulder—always my left, I
don't know why—the round-edged, faceless thing I recognize, now, as
depression is hunkering. Sometimes near, sometimes farther away,
sometimes so far away I can't even see it, but, even when it appears to
have been exiled for good, I know the body's uneven tides may drag it
back within eyeshot, within mindshot, without warning. It, or the idea
of it, is never going to go away: It is part of my basic heart. It is uneven.
It is absolutely, utterly ordinary. It is the way all the me's inside me—
the writer, teacher, woman, wife, friend, daughter—have to live.

I DO NOT WRITE during the bad times; I write on the upswing—but
I have tried to capture what depression is, how it feels. It does not feel

creative. To have depression relieved and creativity resurface—and to write about the periods during which there is neither urge nor ability to create—is both uplifting and disheartening. I revel in having my abilities returned and then using them to articulate, and make a virtual return visit to unfeelingness and wordless abnegation. I use words, when I finally recover them, to speak of what is inexpressible, and I know that, with little, sometimes no warning, my ability to act creatively can be smothered by the body's predilections, by its natural imbalances. It's much like having been mugged from the inside more than once and waiting for the next time. I've spent way too much time trying and failing to outwit what is housed within me.

I know of no way to determine whether the writing itself has changed because of the medications, because my subject demands something different, or simply because a maturing writer's work, if she's lucky, changes. I do know that prescription drugs have both allowed me to write and prevented me from writing, that they have, at their best, opened the black gate long enough for me to experience what I'm left with when the dark thing passes: the me I might be without it. When the medications are right, they lessen depression's influence, let me locate and put to use whatever thinking and writing skills I have. I'm certain they lend me clarity and an ability to look back and sort out the effects of depression—like picking stones from beans—from the parts of myself that may be more enduring. And to articulate what I find. In the midst of depression's blur, that's an impossible task. Depression, often even the effects of medication, is a subject that sets a flame beneath me and lets me see more of what I am and what I hold.

IT IS VERY OFTEN AS THOUGH

We live softly damned, damnation
a small thing built into the body. All
around us: apples and auguries, poems

that speak the small prayers which keep
a weary heart singing. And when we
grasp that small music, incomplete,

approximate, fallible as the body of flesh
that lives to bear it, we can rise up, oh—
we rise and we damn near catch fire.

I've always written erratically: hot for five days or maybe three or even one, for two weeks, three weeks, then not writing at all for a month or for many months. How much of my unevenness is depression? How much just my basic nature? Laziness? Fear? I don't know. Depression has always been there. My ability to concentrate is rotten, that's not new; I get up and walk around, shake myself out as though the physical act of writing is a bodily torment. I write only when a voice or a rhythm or an image roils inside me, and I write best late at night. If I write when I don't *need* to, I write poems that don't need to be read. When I do write, I try to see that the urgency I feel is transferred to the poem itself, that the poem becomes a crucible for that energy. That's always the ideal, anyway.

On most days I am a sedentary person with a sluggish brain and an inactive body. Catching the fire of a poetic impulse is the closest I'll ever come to adventure; no one will make a movie of my life. I lack protagonist potential. I take risks, but on paper. I live inside my head, in the passive, noisy dark. You could sum up most of my life in four still shots: girl/woman sitting, girl/woman lying down. In one set she looks out toward some unnamed elsewhere, her eyes half-closed; in the other, her eyes are shut tight.

There were a few years—high school?—when I walked: up and down El Camino Real, the primary road that runs the length of the San Francisco peninsula, at night, often all night. The boil-up of adolescent fury and confusion had to go somewhere, the loneliness had to take some shape or I'd have flown apart. Depression seemed centrifugal then. Pre-Walkman, pre-iPod, I just walked, hoping to make eye contact with someone, to talk with anyone. Some nights I walked all night, to Palo Alto and home again, an easy twenty miles. Some nights to San Mateo, probably just as far but in the other direction. I was lucky: Despite the occasional eye contact and experience, I never got badly hurt. Perhaps all this is a metaphor. I don't think so.

You could, I suppose, tap into the few peak moments of mayhem in my life, but those are scenes, not plots, and those confrontations are short-lived. There's drama for the moment: it tattoos the heart and flies off until, to my own surprise, way down the proverbial road, it flies back again with its needles and pain, a homing thing. But I am most often a bystander, seldom as innocent as I would like, and, well, at least once, the blatant instigator, though I didn't know it at the time, of disaster.

I manage to remember very little about most things. I remember sensations, emotions, likes, and dislikes. I remember holding back, constantly choking down my impulse to react. I have honed forgetting and silence to near perfection. They make my life more manageable. But I do remember a handful of incidents, quite visually. How reliable are those visions? I don't know. But I will swear to them. And it goes without saying that anything I say now is at least partially untrue: a part-lie by omission, emphasis, angle of approach, or memory's failure. In that, thank god, I am like any other narrator.

My road to prescription drug therapy is long and full of shadows, if not periodically potholed with some real ankle-breakers. The back-story, of course, is longer than the real subject of this essay, the story itself.

THE MEDICATIONS THEMSELVES are mostly a blur. I remember the first was from a GP I trusted. How many years ago? At least fifteen. She understood my problem and in a comradely way prescribed a pair of medications she admitted was old even then, but one that had gotten her through medical school, and she was well into her thirties by the time I saw her. Those pills, whatever they were, made a zombie out of me—speechless, thoughtless. I waited for it to pass; it didn't. By the time I figured out I had to stop them, the doctor had gone off to Central America, I think, to become a missionary. Then other GPs, other pills; nobody back then seemed interested in monitoring the effects of the medications they prescribed. The first I recall by name is Paxil. That worked for a while, though my weight skyrocketed, but its good effects gradually petered out. Then, with my current doctor, a woman fastidious in monitoring my reactions, Prozac; then Prozac with a Wellbutrin chaser; then Celexa, which made my heart beat so hard I thought it would explode in my chest; then Lamictal, which gave me a rash; then Ultram; then Wellbutrin SR 200 mg once a day, then twice a day; then Wellbutrin XL 300 mg. And now a new one: Cymbalta. And here is the body's fickleness once more: the first dose at 60 mg knocked me on my back; I slept for three days. Then half a dose and the change made me hopeful for—I don't know—maybe a week? ten days? Then the slide down began again and back to the sixty. I've been good for a number of months. I'd like to think I'll be this good forever; I consider myself in serviceable condition, sometimes darn good condition. But I know better than to count on it. The body, like the language we use to talk about it, is fluid.

THE MIND, I THINK, is less fluid, and my reason for resisting psychotherapy has been, probably at least at first, conditioning. I managed to live through crisis periods without it. I've convinced myself that being functional rather than miserable is a victory. I'm not brave enough to want to open the doors to the past. I have held so much in for so long that the pressure inside might be too great: I could fly apart and never come back. Why put in jeopardy the progress I've made on my own? And why court grief? Intellectually, I know better—so what keeps me from psychoanalysis now? Some of it's money. And maybe, if I'm kinder than I think, I'm trying not to add to the ways in which I've humiliated my mother. Probably it's my passivity. I've worked out a lot of stuff. But not everything.

SO WHEN I FINALLY come to this woman who can really help me, I say what I've always said: "Hi-I-don't-want-to-talk-I-only-want-the-pills." And then I sit down. She's surely heard this before. We just go over the basics: life, parents, husband, symptoms.

Mine is a blue-collar, when we're lucky, family. When I am born my mother is thirty-eight or -nine, my father almost fifty. In 1949 the late-baby phenomenon is not common. People we don't know think my parents are my grandparents—and these are the rules set down by the parent who speaks: don't ask anybody's business, don't tell anybody ours. Curiosity killed the goddamn cat. Don't get involved. You've got problems? Keep them to yourself—that's what I had to do. I turned out fine. I raised you, didn't I?

My father was born in Kansas in 1900. That's really about all I know of his early life. Dropped out of grade school. As an adult: a lumber man in Santa Cruz, California, an iceman in San Francisco, a some-thing-or-other at the airport, a worker in a suburban ball-bearing fac-tory. There are allusions—not made by him—to a lost love, and a first and second wife. Ma's his third. He's thin, he's bent. He's not strong. His color is always poor. He's ill: part of his stomach has been re-moved. He drinks Schlitz (when he can afford it), and a bottle of Gallo port is hidden beside his workbench in the garage.

My mother was born in San Francisco, probably around 1911. Some-where along the line, her own mother lied to the stepfathers about her daughter's age—to the daughter as well—to make herself seem younger. At least this is what I'm told. And there was the Depression, the furnace ripped out of the wall; leaving school to get a job; there's the restaurant, with allusions to bootlegging in the basement and a whorehouse upstairs. Ma's father is a Spanish Jew who converts to Ca-tholicism; his name is very common; he's a drummer, a traveling sales-man, but I have no idea what he sells. I do not know my mother's mother's name, but perhaps I do—I remember seeing one on the mar-ble in the columbarium by my father's death-condo when I visited Cal-ifornia briefly with my second husband. Though that may have been her mother's mother. As children, Ma and her baby brother were shipped out each summer to relatives in the country. Ma continues to see the train pull away from the station near the orchards, leaving her and her beloved younger brother in the agricultural dust and, when she does, she cries. At ninety-four, she still calls out for her own mother when she is feverish and alone and telephoning me from three thousand miles away. She is angry about her life. Everything about it has been wrong.

I'm born in 1949. And this is the rope ladder I climb down. My DNA.

WHEN I'M EIGHT, I drown. We go to Disneyland though we can't afford it. I hear the discussion through the heating vent: children from happy families go to Disneyland, so we do, too. We are at a motel, one of those long strip motels that were the fashion in the fifties. I am in the shallow end of the pool with my plastic blow-up ring snugged up into my armpits. My mother is on a chaise lounge to my left; my father, on a chaise lounge next to her. They don't seem to see each other. I'm bored, I'm hot, the tension between my parents is giving me a headache, not that I can articulate this at the time—then, it's simply a fact of existence: we are trying to be together, so I have a headache. If you are perfect, I will love you. The sun's hot and the water's cold but there are other kids in the pool obviously doing all the right things. I want to be one of them: I pop up and try a handstand on the pool's floor. I've done it a half-dozen times before and I can do it, so I do. This time, however, the plastic ring slides along my body, up to and around my calves and ankles, holding my feet in the air above the water and my head below. I recall struggling to right myself, to get my head above the literal water, and that's the last I remember before I die.

I have never known such nothingness since, and the memory of that absolute void has stayed with me for fifty years. I often long for it: Nothing. It's impossible to imagine unless you've known it: it is painless and placeless. There is no one there you are likely to disappoint; there is no one there at all, not even you. The next thing I remember is walking past the foot of one of the double beds in our motel room. My father is wringing out his leather wallet and peeling his dollar bills apart and laying them on the radiator to dry. My mother is between the beds, sitting on the edge of one, then standing up; her arms are moving fast in the air about her. She is furious. I have embarrassed them in front of all those people, made a scene, a fuss, and my father, who does not know how to swim, has had to jump in and pull me out. Everybody was watching. I'm inconsiderate, thoughtless, selfish. He could have drowned. It's forty years before I wonder why my mother, who swam at

Fleischaker Pool as a kid in San Francisco, didn't give him a hand. As far as I know, I was dead. I keep this as a reference point. Some years ago, in a rare visit to Ma's, I found a black-and-white postcard of that motel. I can tell you which room door was ours. I can show you where I stood on my hands in the pool when I died.

She throws his ass out, I think, after he wrecks the last car, the green Nash, in Sausalito—or is that the time she drags me to San Francisco on the train and lies to the conductor about my age to get a cheaper ticket and we are gone for days—she shows him!—living in a hotel on Powell and charging everything to the credit card?

By the time I'm in fifth or sixth grade, he's living in a shack behind the Oasis Bar, an old building with a mission façade that faces the railroad tracks. Mine is a tripartite world set within three square blocks. Our house on Flynn faces away from that world. The street behind us—James Street?—is where my school is. And past the school, past the whole length of the green playing field, and past the enormous warehouse of some manufacturer, is Charter Street, the tracks running its length, and the Oasis Bar. I am not supposed to go see him after school, but I do sometimes. I have no idea what we talk about. He probably sweeps some change off his dresser top, buys me a soda and gets himself a beer, and we sit on the edge of the perfectly made bed in that dark, low-ceilinged room—and we drink instead of talk. We can hear the jukebox from the bar. If that isn't the way it is, well . . . I can imagine nothing else. When she finds out, it's another tune altogether, however: Get off your duff and do something if you're bored. Pick yourself up, dust off your behind, and keep moving or you are weak (a moral judgment) or a bum. It's a given there's one bum in the family already, and she took care of him, didn't she? Nobody is going to be weak in her house. She says: There's no such thing as depression, just laziness and dereliction. He's a goddamn drunk. Have a little pride.

When he is sixty-seven and I am sixteen, my mother and I live on the other side of town and he lives in a small cabin in the woods about an hour away. He shoots himself in the head at my mother's house. He's come for Easter; I start the fight because, I say, he was drunk when my girlfriend and I picked him up—and how could he? When I come home from my rage-filled, cathartic drive after the yelling (mine), they are taking him, on a stretcher, from the house. They have to tilt the thing to make it out the front door and around the corner of the narrow porch; they nearly dump him over the railing. I am standing on the grass in the dark with the neighbors trying to make sense of what is going on.

In my twenties I ask (at great expense, because I know she'll never let me hear the end of it) to borrow some money to "see someone." I need help. I'm in crisis. I've been in college and out again, married and divorced, had other bad, sometimes violent, live-in relationships; myriad failures circle my feet. As far as I can see, unless someone helps me straighten myself out, I am done for. My life is a rat's nest; I have thrown it away.

> and lo! she was wacky as a toad
> and would not move from her bed,
>
> blinked a lightless room, shades
> down like blades, o! weeks, she
>
> thought in couplets, two burps:
> the world folds up again—set
>
> the awful world away—it lived
> in a place beneath the bed, it
>
> lived in a place above the bed,
> her lines, when she had lines,
>
> when she had poems—she had
> no poems—black ducks running,
>
> stoats & swine, so down she'd never
> rise, o! ask, help anything me

It takes her only a moment to say no—No, she isn't lending me money to give to some shrink who is going to tell me that she's done everything wrong. I simply am not bright enough to work it out myself at the time. I understand neither the state in which she lives her life nor how hard it is for her to keep redefining the world in order to keep herself on top of it. And besides, she's worked on the switchboard of a big county hospital, and it is common knowledge that all psychiatrists' pants are too short and they are crazy themselves to boot. I'm not blaming her for my failure to get help. We were both doing the best we could, the same thing we always did and continue to do: what we need to do to stay alive. But, in a rash moment in my mid-fifties, I tell her that I am taking antidepressants. She says, "Well, it runs on both sides of the family." I remind her of what she said when I was a kid: no such thing, laziness, dereliction. "Yes, of course, that's what I said," she says, "but you know what I meant." Her tone speaks whole worlds of impatience.

MY DEPRESSION, as a middle-aged adult is nonspectacular, a dark weight. It takes the form of acedia, of lethargy, of inertia. A spiritless-ness and disengagement varying from deadening—shapeless, muscle-less, Gary Larson's *Far Side* depiction of the boneless chicken ranch—to manageable. In my youth, melancholy, yes, and wild frustration, but seldom now. Now a resignation, a leaning into, a wish to simply melt away, a longing to simply let the body's liquors follow gravity's dictate and mingle, at the minutest level, with the dirt below. And in the throes I can find no meaning unless darkness itself is a meaning.

I am told that depression is anger turned inward. And perhaps so. But yelling, all those outward manifestations of anger, have not worked for me in the past and are not available to me in the present. A few times, in my youth, I gave breaking things a shot, a plate here, a cup there, but destruction releases nothing for me except the additional be-reavement of loss and a huge sense of foolishness. Instead, I eat it. My default mode is to shut up and shut down. I am so busy trying to please, so busy quashing any impulse that may run counter to what is allowed, that I no longer recognize what I really want or feel. Once, after a visit to my mother—in my forties, I think—I remained virtually silent for nearly three weeks. I wasn't being surly: the thought/speech-producing mechanism had simply closed up shop. What was there to say? Nothing—there was nothing at all to say. Don't question, don't argue, don't explain—and if you yell at me, you don't love me. Don't say a word except in delight or gratitude.

The urge toward suicide? I don't think it's due to example, though that's certainly there. Escape was on my mind long before my father carried through—and the answer to his mess, made clear at the time, is, once the floor and walls are cleaned up, ignore it. Don't talk about it. It is *so* not talked about that we don't even have to talk about not talking about it.

> Where the bullet broke the skull there is a hole. A small
> hole. Almost neat. And you are lying on your back. The
> skull is still, your hands. The box you lie in, still. For the
> first time I see the whole of you. For the first time you are
> not walking away, your bent back a wall of going away.
> And I have nothing to tell you. And nothing to hold back.
> The world is still out here. You are still alone. The women

of your life still don't know how to say goodbye. And
when the whole world of you is ash of ash, thirty years behind the marble wall, you begin to speak to me: bullets,
you say, are nothing. Ash is nothing. You say: look how
your blood is the bearer of such news.

He dies when I'm nearly seventeen. I write a short essay about it at
thirty-four. At fifty-one, he begins to pop up in my poems. No one's
more surprised than I am. And he's lingering. That thing in the heart
again. A seventeen-year locust.

In the arrogance of the body I know you,
tunnel I stumble through (room I sleep in).

In this way, we died both. (One speaks over
white paper, the other swept like sand beneath

a sea.) You are the poem I keep writing.
Dear Sir, I still carry your gun in my hand.

This is where chemistry and calamity collide.

Does wishing for death count? Because I'm absolutely certain I do
that. But wishing probably doesn't count. And if I'm honest, neither
does the night I sit at the side of the tracks. I don't think I am in high
school yet. I am waiting for the train; I am miles from home. The despair is nameless except for *loneliness* or *desperation,* and those may be
products of hindsight. That night I believe I'd give anything not to feel
the way I've felt for so long. The train, of course, doesn't come. When
the sky breaks into its morning palette, I walk home, wash my hair, and
go to school. Would I have done it? I don't think so. But I can't really
know. Decisions are made in an instant.

I USED TO THINK she was the bad guy, he was the victim. After mar-
rying my own older-man-alcoholic, my second husband, I'm not so sure
anymore; at least not as dogmatically, arrogantly certain. I understand a
little more about disappointment now. Besides, my story turned out a
lot better. Yes, I married my father, a kind, quiet alcoholic fourteen years
my senior, who, for ten years out of our twenty-five, let me believe he
was dying. Maybe he was. But I was incorrigibly stupid. And, because of
my inaptitude for acting on my anger, I stayed on and we came through
it. I know what a fuzzy bastard truth is. And mine isn't the only story.

When the slide down begins, and I am able to recognize it as such, I am terrified—the prospects of another wrong prescription drug, or of just another disappointment, or perhaps of running out of possibilities, of having run through the entire medicine cabinet of the industry and coming up depressed. Depression with no outlook for its lifting? That's where I was when the train didn't come—but it has come for more than just a couple of others I know.

THE SUICIDES

I won't name them for you, or count them,
each one a door, and the house fallen down.
A wall is a small, simple history. And falling
is everywhere. Imagine the hinged eyes close

or are closed—no, sleep is nothing like
the death. Still, no one dies of bullets
or the belt slung around the neck. No one
dies in the black wade of the sea, not one

by the train, the insatiable train—but
the blurred curve of space about the body,
the space of the body itself, its prodigal
boundary, think of that. What dies before
the heavy body follows? Rattle the skull,
the breath, the will. The walls are sighing.
There is a violent wind kissing the latch.
And there are days I do not know my name.

My grace: that the chemicals make me erratic even in wanting to die and that I am far too cowardly and afraid of pain to kill myself now. I am nearly certain of this. But I will nonetheless die one of these days, by my hand, another's hand, or no hand at all.

It is as simple as this: no thing surrendered
in the woods last night. Everything surrenders.

So, while I still have choice, I, in a manner of speaking, choose.

The pills didn't help. And they helped.
The writing blew away. The life laid down

DEPRESSION AND THE ORDINARY

and sang a low melody distorted by the sun.
    And continued. The life swallowed

the sun and went on. Out there, the highway
    had a voice like birds in a cavern. Out there,

the timberland burned like another tongue.
    (The birds would not trill. The flame gave no

light.) And nothing from the news was willing
    to save her. The relic was her self, old

fingerbone, divided, horizontal. When
    the second illness leaned over her, a dark

tumbled to its side, a snippet of light let in. When
    that second illness hunkered down, enough

glimmer blew through to see—then dark like
    a lever to raise her. The choice of default,

of omission, of *take the air in, then let it go.*

IN THE MOVIE OF MY LIFE, I'm sitting on a covered porch. The house is white and has a great many rooms of varying sizes and contours. Its rugs are threadbare and many of the doors are swollen shut. The windows are cracked and cloudy. There is no other house in view. Some days, the sky is the color of a storm; the wind can be humorless. The black gate swings back and forth, open and shut. So far, there is no latch that can hold it for long. When it swings, anything can come in or can leave, and the swinging is at the mercy of the weather, ordinary weather. A bent nail, a hammer. A bottle of pills. Right now, the dark thing is far away.

Eleven

FOOD FOR THOUGHT

CATERINA EPPOLITO, MA, MFA

IN ALL MY YEARS of practicing therapy, I have never had a client say that she or he wants to begin therapy to become more creative. On the other hand, I have had a client who began treatment because he was too creative. A child told a panicked teacher that he heard voices. When I worked with this child, I found out that these voices were just a creative adaptation of imaginary playmates.

Like my clients, when I entered treatment, it was not to become more creative. In hindsight, my mind had become far too creative; its unconscious creative solution to the shock of my father abandoning his family was for me to develop anorexia in my late adolescence.

To understand how creativity and psychotherapy are related, you have to go beneath the surface of my poetry, just as you must look beyond the surface presentation of anorexia to know that it is not about weight or physical appearance. To understand how psychotherapy enhanced my creativity, you must understand more deeply the illness for which I sought treatment. Like the threads of the three fates, the anorexia, psychotherapy, and creativity are intrinsically tangled.

By twenty-three, I had been hospitalized, had sought treatment, had received a BS degree in psychology, and had earned an MFA in creative writing. By then I thought that the disease was behind me. But before I left treatment, the clinical director of the program did not sing my praises but almost scolded me, "Deny it if you want. I'll be seeing you again. The anorexia is ingrained in your mind." In that moment, I hated her for saying it. I didn't like the idea that she was telling me that I was not cured; I was merely in remission. Then, glancing up from her chart from her faux leather chair, looking at my academic background, and almost as an afterthought, she casually remarked, "Poetry, it figures; writing can't get more anorexic than that."

I looked up in shock at the metaphor that compared my poetry to a destructive disease. How dare she compare my writing to an illness! Now, I realize that therapists often try to make metaphoric connections between the person's diagnosis and the client's life, believing that the illness is a physical manifestation of a mental process. Then, it was a revelation I didn't want to hear. For five years I had worked hard to rebuild my life from the devastation of the illness. I had returned to college, earned a master's degree, moved across the country, and rebuilt relationships. While I was free of its blatant physical manifestations, it never occurred to me that I could still be psychologically a closet anorexic. Like being a dry drunk, I still had the same mental processes that I'd had when I was ill; I merely sublimated the obsession into a more positive, socially acceptable form—poetry. While there is no doubt that writing poetry is more positive than being anorexic and dying, my therapist pointed out that this clever defense mechanism allowed me to be rooted in my disease. After all, the symptoms of restriction, the drive for perfection, obsession, and need to control were all there.

Poetic form is an anorexic form of writing. Literally, poetry is the thinnest form of writing. Poetry is so thin that by its very definition it cannot fit across the page. So instead of restricting calories, I was restricting words. Instead of controlling what was left on my plate, I was controlling what was left on the page. Instead of spending hours trying to rid myself of extra food, I was spending hours fiddling with words trying to rid myself of verbal excess. Still there was that obsessive drive for perfection with each additional revision.

Poetry is as full of forms as anorexia is filled with rules. Just as there were self-restrained rules to eat only certain foods, there were poetic forms using rhyme and meter that ruled out certain words and allowed others. Certain formal forms, like the sestina or the sonnet, had such strict, regimented patterns that it seemed crazy to try to imprison my emotional expressions within them.

In the beginning, anorexia is not about emotional expression; it is about emotional restriction. One of the first things an anorexic person learns in treatment is that the disease isn't about the food or the weight. Food and weight are only metaphors. They are the medium through which the anorexic person communicates what she feels is unspeakable. Anita Johnston, psychotherapist and author of *Eating by the Light of the Moon,* writes that the eating disorder is something that she used to deal with the emotional distress of feeling different, misunderstood, unaccepted, and overwhelmed. She needed to consider the possibility that the eating disorder may have been a reasonable choice, considering the limited options, resources, or coping skills available during a crisis in her life.

Like the Echo from Greek mythology, an anorexic person often doesn't have a voice of her own. She often mimics the words of what she perceives others want to hear. Likewise, she feels what others want or allow her to feel. She denies other emotions in the same way she denies her own hunger. I, for example, hid my sadness and depression when my father left. I tried to purge those feelings by fasting. Fasting numbed the emotional pain, because the hunger that caused obsessions with food and weight distracted me from the more painful emotional issues. When given the choice to obsess over a suicidal thought or a carrot stick, the mind chooses a carrot stick because it is safer and less painful.

In a similar way, in my poetry, I wrote in other people's voices because they were safer and less painful to work through than my own voice. I didn't value my own voice. Projecting my emotions onto others, I chose to write in the voices of various historical or mythical characters. I wrote poems in the voices of Virginia Woolf, Van Gogh, Freud's Anna O, Thoreau, Civil War soldiers, Walt Whitman, Echo, Eurydice, and Persephone, to name a few. I used their words taken from journals, letters, and essays to explore my own feelings of grief, loneliness, and fear of madness. I found it safer to explore my psychological turmoil in characters or voices other than my own.

In my isolation, I was looking to Virginia Woolf's writing to find another person to understand and explain my experience. "The Jarring" is a sonnet derived from Woolf's journals recollecting her childhood visits to the seashore. The childhood memory of collecting moths is supposed to foreshadow her famous essay "Death of a Moth," which grapples with existential issues of life and death, and her later depression. Like Woolf, as a child I, too, looked to nature in fascination and awareness of life's beauty and life's cruelty. The last stanza of "The Jarring" :

Confined to bed, she hears them again,
their white wings falling quietly as feminine endings.
They whisper, we are *little or nothing*.
Jarred, without any edges to cling to,
a moth rests on her pencil's thin ledge.

The closest I ever came to revealing my own personal history was in the poem entitled "Echo," in which the starving nymph of Greek mythology, heartbroken by Narcissus, is sent to a modern-day mental hospital. I had been hospitalized for three months as I recovered from anorexia. It was a teaching hospital, so most of the patients would get more than their fair share of testing, assessment, and observation. Yet, the more all these people tried to get to know me, the less I felt they understood me.

The poem was structured to mimic the rhythms of "This Is the House That Jack Built" because of the echo of the words. The repetition of the form creates a slight echo as it moves from stanza to stanza, and the last stanza shrinks away to one line just as Echo shrinks away until only her voice remains.

ECHO

This is the young lady who lives in one room.
The door has a window. There's wire in the window.
Someone has taken the keys and locked her up.

Each door has a lock. Glass objects are forbidden.
Here is the nurse who wears only one glove.
She is inspecting the bed. She will not turn it down.
. . . .
"Where are the petals?" asks the assistant
who has studied Rorschach. He is making a list.
He writes his own notes for his book.
. . . .

This is the nurse watching her eat,
counting the peas she hides under a lettuce leaf.
She writes it down on an unused paper napkin.

This is the doctor nodding his head. Is he falling asleep?
He has lost his watch under the bed.
He scrawls a prescription down on a slip.

She cuts diamonds from the folded sheets.
The small flakes are falling down,
falling in sheets of invisible snow.

Her reflection frosts the window's glass.

On the surface of the poem, the psychological professionals are seen in a frosty light. So how could psychotherapy enhance creativity other than giving me characters to parody?

First of all, without psychotherapy the poems wouldn't have been written. Anorexia is so consuming that one doesn't have the energy or strength to be creative or prolific. During the progression of the illness, I had begun a journal with the idea that I could capture on the page what I was mentally experiencing. But as the illness became more and more severe, my writing diminished in the same way my body did. The scariest part of this was that it wasn't a choice. I remember staring at the page trying to put a sentence together. I couldn't concentrate enough to think anything more than a basic thought. My mind did not have enough fuel to write creatively, so my entries in the journal literally dwindled to a list of foods followed by their calories. Without therapy, I wouldn't have recovered enough to write poetry.

Second, by making me look at where my beliefs about myself came from, psychotherapy made me better able to evaluate why I wanted to be a writer instead of something else someone else wanted me to be. While I wasn't exactly happy going through a "midlife crisis" at twenty, I am grateful that I was able to devote a number of years of my life to writing and teaching instead of jumping into a career that became so instilled in me that I forgot why I had chosen it. I put off going to graduate school in clinical psychology to write and teach. During this time, I was symptom free and at my most prolific. I would eventually return to the field of psychology, but it wouldn't be without its hurdles. I began to relapse during my second year of graduate school as I focused on psychology instead of poetry.

I began to realize that I had a problem when a child in the supermarket check-out line commented on my thirty containers of yogurt and no other food. Once I got home, I made an appointment to see a counselor who specialized in eating disorders. I chose her because of her background in nutrition. I had thought that I just needed to be told the benefits of fat to overcome my fear of eating fat. I was surprised when she asked me to come back the following week. I would soon realize that my issues went much deeper than a simple phobia about eating fats.

Collecting background information, she was intrigued that while I was writing, I was, for the most part, without symptoms. She asked me how I felt when I was writing poetry. I think she was expecting me to say that it was freeing and liberating. (Therapists often suggest writing between sessions as a way of expressing or containing feelings while not in session. Most people report feeling relief as they do so.) Instead, I likened writing poetry to trying to write in a straightjacket.

We explored why I didn't tend to write in freer forms, such as journaling or no-send letters. I explained that these forms tended not to work for me. I had read the journals of Virginia Woolf and the letters of

Van Gogh; their writing had vision, images, passion, and eloquence. I noticed that they rarely wrote about their innermost turmoil, which would later lead to their mythologized suicides.

Looking back on my journals I see a mind tormented by obsession and depression, page after page. There are descriptions of anguish, and I, the author, am trapped in that mindset. Writing it down made the pain more concrete and the thoughts far too real.

I would explain to my therapist that the process of writing poetry forced me to transform the pain. It forced me to cast the hot lead of my formless thoughts into pewter plates of poetry. In my poem "Prodigal Dinners," ironically a half-portioned sestina, I describe the emotional cutoff I felt with my father. There is a loose allusion to the parable of the Prodigal Son.

> What separates us more than weather?
> The shifting of our plates of lettuce
> or the faults of California's plates? Both leave sand
> on the tongue as if they were crumbs of stale biscuits
> or words crumbled into your answering machine. I see
> you wave the waiter down with nothing
>
> but the downdraft of your hand. It's nothing
> for you to mention our humid weather,
> regardless of the lukewarm currents of opposite seacoasts.
> You order your wine. I break champagne biscuits
> until they're ruins of Babel or steeples of sand
> cathedrals. We are more civil when there is an ocean between us,
>
> because it's harder to see what isn't here. Let's
> not bicker over biscuits, a basket of white lies.
> The distance, the silence, is nothing
> that a dinner in St. Augustine can't cure. "The Sea,"
> by Debussy, plays on the radio. Did George Sand
> and Chopin discuss the weather,
>
> the cloud-like biscuits crumbling over the sea?
> Nothing but fronts filled their discussions. There's the texture
>   of sand,
> the sustenance of lettuce in our weather.

I found something healing in forming beautiful images from words I had soldered together. I described the process of writing poetry as making a leaded-glass window out of the broken pieces of my life. In the process, the broken pieces mend into something treasured. The raw edges don't cut because they are now encased in metal of words and form. Through this creative process the raw shards of pain are transformed into images so vivid and so deliberated that these created images become as real as the actual memory. Linda Garro and James Hillman's research shows that memories are best understood as reconstructions of the past and not as literal reproductions of the past, making our life stories told in therapy "healing fictions."[1]

In this way, psychotherapy is a parallel process to the process of writing poetry. The ability to reexamine, reimagine, and to reframe past events is a powerful therapeutic tool available in both poetry and therapy. Harlene Anderson writes that, in the dialogue, new themes and new stories develop. Psychotherapy is the process of saying the unsaid— the development of new narratives. From these narratives new meanings arise, and in turn, these new histories give rise to change.[2] According to therapist James Hillman, in the therapeutic process, a client's past is retold and finds a new internal coherence. In the poetic process the writer's words find new coherence as they are forced to be contained and reframed.[3]

Freud believed that the creative process is the internalization of the child's play process. Just as the child uses physical toys to help play out events that are too painful to speak directly, the writer's process is to play with words as if they were toys, picking one up, throwing it across the page, while arranging and revising.

In "Prodigal Dinners" I made the brave leap into first person, daring to describe the estrangement of my father, which became a catalyst for the development of anorexia. In the original memory, my father controlled all of my life events, but as the events were depicted in poetry, it was I who would control and recast the mood and tone. This feeling of power and mastery led me to recast myself from archetypal victim to archetypal heroine.

In the beginning of therapeutic work, I thought that my father's leaving was the sole cause of the anorexia. But I would learn later that the scaffolding for the anorexic structure began in childhood.

Not only did my poetry move out of the third person into the personal ownership of the first person, but I also began writing poems that went deep and deeper into memory. As I processed earlier and earlier events in therapy, my poetry examined earlier periods of my life. Freud, when writing about his first memories, saw them through a foggy screen, thereby calling the earliest memories "screen memories." Screen memories are a scattering of incoherent images that represent and express a core emotion to be processed by the therapist. Since my poetry often formed itself around particular images, I decided to play with the idea; I would try to write coherent poems from the scattered images of memory of my great grandmother's funeral, when I was four years old.

The poem written from "screen memories" is in the elegy "Adoration Downward Falling," named after a prayer in my children's missal. It starts with "God was still in the windless sky" and ends with the following:

> The music box had stopped
> a small solemn girl from feeding
> her circle of six wooden chickens.
>
> Down fell soft as sleet
> through the wire windows
> of the hen house.
>
> In the hushed house,
> I was allowed to hold
> A blue-tipped carnation.
>
> Mother's face was veiled.
> through the prism
> of the flower's plastic casket,
>
> its slender, green vase,
> Jesus on the crucifix
> became the green copper gargoyle
>
> who slept in the eves of a children's bible.
> Through the petal of the rose window,
> Snow sank like small paper wings.

The poem begins with a split perception of God, who is an absent comforter. In the line, "God is still in the windless sky," "still" can be interpreted in contrasting ways: "still" defined as actionless, or "still" defined as "being present." In the image in the penultimate stanza, Christ on the crucifix is compared to a gargoyle. A gargoyle could be a comforter, because it was believed to keep away evil spirits, but it could be a scary, tormenting demon creature in its physical appearance to a child.

In analysis, I began to wonder where this perception that God could be a frightening creature came from. At the time of my grandfather's death, I worried whether he would go to heaven, because I didn't know if he had gone to confession. Hoping to comfort myself, I tried picturing him in heaven. Unfortunately, in fear, the images in my mind were of him in fire with angels falling into demons hour after hour, night after night. I tried praying. If I got the words wrong, I would have to start all over again. I said Hail Marys and Our Fathers in patterns of ten.

I was afraid I was crazy, so I kept this as a secret. Because of the shame, I wouldn't be diagnosed as having obsessive-compulsive disorder until I was twenty-two. In my poem "When Angels Were Wingless," in the last tercet of a sestina, an obsessive-compulsive poetry form in which the six end words of each stanza are repeated six times in six patterns ending in a tercet using all six words, I write,

> . . . outside silence
> Peels the bark from the birch. The wind uncovers
> The rose of new skin. Stillness is the only silence;
> birches scrub the sky with scuffed wings,
> razing the prayers no snow can cover.

Here nature is personified as needing purification through endless ablutions, the action of scrubbing to the point of bleeding or peeling away of old skin. My eventual anorexic obsession would replace this childhood ritual of purification.

I learned in therapy that anorexia began for me as a spiritual fast. At the time, I was overwhelmed by my father's leaving and my mother's deepening depression. Growing up with the stories of fasting saints, I asked God to give me the strength to make me strong enough to cope. As the disease progressed, I was convinced that I didn't deserve to eat because I wasn't a good enough person. In my striving to be good, I told myself that I was bad and needed to be better. After all, one needs to be humble before God. Soon, the anorexic thought process convinced me that I didn't deserve to live because I never should have been alive in the first place. The doctors had told my parents when I was born, at the premature weight of two pounds, with slight cerebral palsy, that I had a one-in-ten chance of survival.

Understanding the roots of the eating disorder, I grew furious with God and others around me. This was a new and scary feeling because anger in my family was forbidden. I have no memory of my parents ever fighting. Because I was still new to the open expression of anger, I looked to the poem "Fever 103," written by Sylvia Plath after one of her husband's affairs. I borrowed Plath's structure by replacing her words with their opposite to create the original scaffolding. The resulting poem, "Stillborn," captures my anger of still being born with an "abnormal" body.

> Yes, I'm thought
> christened
> in a hospital gown.
>
> Its well-worn pain
> covers your pain
> and, I, the ice child
>
> open my mouth
> like an orchid
> in sterile air.
> Mother, Brine Angel,
> you fed me salt,
> chicken broth, water
>
> .   .   .   .
> Now, see how finitely delicate
> my skin can be
> when carefully sloughed.

Unlike in my first poems, here much of the emotional restriction is gone, as is any sign of meter or rhyme. This is free verse in the truest form. Still, it gives voice to my desire to free myself of my physical form. When recovering from an eating disorder, the last part of the disorder to remain is body image distortion, which is the symptom most impervious to therapy—as seen here, where the skin is cast off.

At first glance it is hard to believe that this poem demonstrates progress in therapy. But for a person who grew up denying anger as an emotion, the open expression of emotion without fear of reprisal is a therapeutic breakthrough. Repression of anger is not uncommon for a person with my diagnosis. Verbal outward expression of negative emotions is a standard treatment goal in the field of eating disorders.

Finally, one of the treatment goals that occurs in the last stages of therapy and is seen as a true measure of recovery, more than any maintenance of a normal weight, is the ability to love another with communication that is both verbal and physical. My most recent poems deal with these issues. They also present a positive image of the body. In a love poem, "The Sound," there is not the silent cry of anorexia.

It is not the half-rest
of the crest, or the low crescendo of sea.

It is not the waves' cursive strokes
or the windfallen wings, the feathers of foam,

or the quavering of the lighthouse light.
It is quieter—

The wind wills its signature to the waves.
The moons long O moves

upon the sea in the white refrains of waves,
like a cymbal

in the 9th symphony. As we wake,
The morning takes a thousand shapes

where a single voice repeats
over the letters

of a never written note which clatters
over the chatter of the kitchen's

dishes. Your words, like melodies
wander . . .

What more than the ceaseless sounds
of everydayness bind us?

It is the dullness, the dampened sound of love
quietly ebbing.

Although I didn't like a therapist's revelation that poetry was a continuation of my anorexic thinking, it was true. Although my body had physically recovered, my poems were full of constraint, restriction, rules, and obsession. They were lacking emotion, freedom, personal ownership, and intimacy. As I progressed in therapy, my writing became more creative: first, I learned to take ownership of my experiences; second, I changed from writing about historical and mythological characters to my own personal experiences, to writing in the first person rather than hiding behind the third-person pronoun; third, I learned to become comfortable with a full spectrum of emotions ranging from rage to passion; and finally, when I explored my earliest years in therapy, I also explored them in poetry.

What I discovered through the therapeutic process was that anorexia was not a hunger for thinness but a hunger to be heard. I had been so afraid of speaking my feelings that I had made them physical, so physical that even my poetry resembled anorexia. Psychotherapy gave my work weight as it gained emotion, intimacy, and openness.

Freud believed that progress in therapy was demonstrated by the ability to work and love well. Along similar lines, Virginia Woolf once wrote that "to live well one must eat, drink and sleep well"; but now I pause before using another's words, knowing the importance of owning my own voice. In psychotherapy I learned that to live well, one must eat, think, and love well.

NOTES

1. Linda C. Garro, "Narrative Representations of Chronic Illness Experience: Cultural Models of Illness, Mind, and Body Stories Concerning TMJ," *Social Science Medicine* 38, no. 6 (1994): 755–88. James Hillman, *Healing Fiction* (Woodstock, CT: Spring Publications, 1983).

2. Harlene D. Anderson, "Collaborative Language Systems: Toward a Postmodern Therapy," in *Integrating Family Therapy*, ed. Richard H. Mikesell, DonDavid Lusterman, and Susan H. McDaniel, 27–44 (Washington, DC: American Psychological Association, 1995).

3. Hillman, *Healing Fiction*, 10.

Twelve

FROM BOG TO CRYSTAL

BARBARA F. LEFCOWITZ, PhD

So let us, after all, pay our respects
to this Couch as we would the pastel madness
of a favorite aunt, frescoes with fading angels.

— LEFCOWITZ, "FREUD'S COUCH"

How dare Dr. S. damn my poetry, especially my published poetry, with faint praise? The first time I presented him with some of my work, his response, expressed in a lackluster manner a few days later, was that he "liked the poems but did not love them." Surely these were words from the devil, not any angel, fading or not.

And how dare he dismiss my work in such a glib, even arrogant manner, when I had already published three well-received poetry collections and won a coveted fellowship from the National Endowment for the Arts, among other honors? All on my own, no less—without any workshops or mentors, even active discouragement of creative writing when I studied for my doctorate in English literature. Worse, the distinction between *love* and *like* evoked a memory of a Herbert Gold novel about a failing marriage, thus reminding me, however obliquely, of the cracks in my own marriage. Had Dr. S. actually read those poems? True, some were on the dark side: was he trying to exploit that darkness to stress how much therapeutic illumination I needed from him?

I felt so shattered I nearly abandoned the therapy, which had already gotten off to a rough start, partly because I had been in treatment with another doctor, who had finally convinced me there was nothing more he could offer me. I was fifty years old at the time and for most of my life had struggled with chronic depression and obsessional anxieties, including hypochondria. I had made some progress with this first therapist, who encouraged my writing and art work but did not see it as an integral part of the therapy. Clearly the gains were neither sufficient nor of sufficient depth: my chronic depression quickly intensified, along with panic attacks that overwhelmed me when driving the Beltway to work and teaching my classes, thus threatening my career as a professor of English. And I was writing little—nothing worth saving.

My former therapist recommended Dr. S., who had a strong literary background and, unlike himself, specialized in psychoanalysis; I took the risk of contacting him despite my memory of having a crush on him many years back, when we had sat two rows apart in a high school creative writing class. We never actually spoke with each other, and, mercifully, I had swept the stories and poems written for that class, his as well as mine, into a black hole somewhere in 1950s Brooklyn. Over the years I had forgotten him, as well.

But I suspect that memory persisted unconsciously, my adolescent fantasies arousing unrealistic expectations that my "love" would no longer be unrequited. Thus, I did not abandon Dr. S. and slowly began to find the therapy more challenging, even exciting, than my previous experience, despite a number of painful interludes. As I write this essay I am still in treatment and still writing both poetry and prose at a pace that often arouses that all too common fear of silence—something I have yet to resolve, a fear paradoxically intensified by the close bond between poetry and therapy that ultimately developed. (More later on the advantages and disadvantages of this bond.) And so, despite his initial dismissal of my work, I began to write poetry again, and after a few months I began to present new poems to Dr. S., hoping that he would find me gifted to the point of brilliance. Such a hope, however narcissistic, served to rejuvenate the creative process.

Likewise Dr. S.'s emphasis on the unconscious: about a year into treatment I wrote a long poem in response to a news story about the body of an old woman that had been excavated, brain intact, from burial eight thousand years ago in a Florida peat bog. Now she was finally "giving up her secrets," according to the *Washington Post*. Because of the poem's length, I quote here only a few lines:

> With delicate chisels
> they pick off bits of clinging peat,
> probe her brain's double cage,
> its outer bonework, inner lacery of nerves.

Later I express a wish to be recombined, made one again. And though I identify myself through my Peat Bog Lady persona as "an ambassador of death / without portfolio," I also note her wish to be revived, though she will probably not be able to survive except deep inside me "until my last brainlight flickers." Finally, I move away from the persona and express in my own voice regrets for frustrated ambitions I could not, now in my fifties, attain. Yet I find comfort imagining that "someday I will become the Peat Bog Lady" once and for all,

> my brain excavated from under the skull
> of some bald planet
>
> . . . . . .
>
> and all those strangers greeting me
> as once I was greeted under bright lights.

In retrospect, I realize that I was attracted to the subject matter because of its associations with the unconscious mind, the dangers of its exposure under clinical light notwithstanding, and, on a more personal level, with the plight of my mother, who had suffered a psychotic breakdown shortly after retiring to Florida. On another level, I recognize now that it was both a template and a road map for the years of therapy ahead, the poem containing some of my frequent poetic and psychological concerns, like my lifelong need for the admiration of others, my Plathian obsession with death (these days considerably shorn of romanticized hysteria), and my fear that if anything good were to happen, it would soon be canceled out—by reality, or more likely by the strongly pessimistic habits of my mind, habits still not transmuted as much as I would wish. Dr. S. expressed great interest in the poem and, thankfully, did not force it into a psychoanalytic Procrustean bed. But mirabile dictu: my usually reserved therapist actually commented about the brilliance of the images, which led simultaneously not only to restored confidence in my writing ability but also to enhancement of the growing bond between us. Was therapy the cause and increased writing the effect, or vice versa? Such a clear-cut distinction is impossible, because cause and effect were becoming mutual.

Still, other poems written about the same time reveal, I now realize, the persistence of my angry disappointment with Dr. S., despite his luminous credentials. Likely the anger followed a resurfacing of my adolescent fantasies about him. But anger, too, can stimulate creativity, which in turn can offer relief from the turmoil of anger. A key poem in this context, "The Guide," was drawn from a vivid dream. Both dream and poem, which take place in Machu Picchu, Peru, a place I was not to visit until fifteen years later, express and ultimately transcend my rage. Briefly, I am impatient to climb the famous limestone steps, but the guide—doubtless Dr. S.—is loitering at the base camp, more interested in carousing with his cronies than leading the way up. After a number of angry questions, I rebel and take off on my own, leap over the steps, and glide through the air steadily upward, far above the other tourists and, most important, the guide. My triumphant ascent has been difficult, but at the end I am singing "so loud my head is filled with music."

Another poem stimulated by anger at that time expresses the fantasy of plunging my hands into the partly torn pockets of a man's coat; finding nothing but the wrappers of old words, I nonetheless enter the coat and walk inside its shape, exploring its many layers, until I come to a deeply hidden but shining inner core, similar to the most inward figure of a Russian Matryoshka doll. That final image prefigures a more favorable sense of self, the first of many such (though there would be no dearth of dark lines to come). "The Stone," a poem invoked by a mellowing anger, even dares to imagine the lifting of my neurotic symptoms, with all the attendant ambivalence: the embedded stone, once excised, turns out to be ludicrously small after all, no weightier than my passel of personal quirks. I do not recall Dr. S.'s responses to the preceding poems, except an intensification of his encouragement: no more mention of the dichotomy between like and love.

Ah, but the monster within, a favorite construct of Dr. S.'s, was still far from extirpated—if indeed it ever could be, except perhaps in part, or, more realistically, defanged and thus viewed with less alarm about its power to threaten my stability of mind and body. The notion of a monster was both intriguing and confusing, provoking an effort to control it, at least in words. The narrator of "Naming the Monster" does not, however, conjure any monolithic megamonster; rather, she breaks it down, one means of weakening its power, a process particularly encouraged by analysis. But to make the idea more concrete—an essential part of the creative process—the narrator imagines and names a series of submonsters, an essential prelude toward a later synthesis of its assumed threats. Naming is also a process of distinguishing between hitherto vague anxieties. Indeed, naming itself is a primitive anxiety—and Adam may have been the world's first poet. The monster can be given more names than a Spanish contessa, prelude to its splitting into many different monsters, who gather to map out their strategies, among them

> bird-monsters to snatch the words right off our plates,
> fish-monsters to dam our most fluent sentences,
> goat-monsters to shred our stories and eat them.

BARBARA F. LEFCOWITZ

But naming in itself is not enough; the monsters' potential ravages are linked particularly with writing, whether sentences, poems, or whole stories. So the therapist him- or herself might turn out to be the monster who dulls the edges of creativity by overanalysis, a fear familiar to many poet-patients, but fortunately not a habit of Dr. S.'s, despite his psychoanalytic orientation. Also, by substituting the pronoun *one* for *I*, I try to establish distance from my own symptoms: a necessity Dr. S. repeatedly asserted.

Indeed, a broadening of the creative process to include both reaching beyond the self and melding fragments of self and world became increasingly frequent in my writing at this time. By taking this step, I began to recognize that breaking down not only reduced anxiety but also led to a process of synthesis, with often surprising results, in both poetry and experiments with prose villanelles as well as my own inventions, a series of "Triads" that juxtapose loosely related objects, persons, or facts to explore the subtle links between them, for example, "Pearls, Rain, Eggs" and "Rope, Pockets, the Bidet." I included autobiographical material, but the syntheses dealt more with relating the personal to the world of objects and ideas. This new splitting and joining was related in part to the free association of the therapeutic hour, but in a more controlled manner. Even more surprising than the content, despite the experimental forms, most of the thirty or so such works were published, a welcome sign that my literary concerns were not as isolated as I had thought. (At that time, I also began to work on a number of mixed-media collages.)

Still I complained often during those therapeutic hours about the social isolation consequent upon my painful divorce after more than thirty years of marriage. I do not believe that pain in and of itself triggers the creative imagination; indeed, pain usually overwhelms both the imagination and the creative act. Yet poems and stories I wrote after the divorce, though often filled with extreme rage—for example, a story in which I place my ex and his mistress in the ovens of Auschwitz—helped shape some of the pain and transmute my fears of isolation into the solitude essential for any creative work. "The Embrace," the concluding poem in *The Minarets of Vienna,* asserts the beginning of an acceptance, even a love, of my solitary self. Or should I say it *prefigures* such an acceptance, a distinction implicit and often confusing in any coalition between poetry and therapy? True, Dr. S. and I argue till this day about the distinction between prefiguration and wish-fulfillment fantasies. Clearly he, like any therapist, prefers to engender actual rather than potential psychological changes.

In the years before my next book (*A Hand of Stars*, 1999), the rage induced by the divorce led to an even greater concern with transcending the self than noted previously, a gradual shift to a creative detachment that would enable me to realize that there are more things on heaven and earth than the crumbling of a long marriage and, in turn, contribute much more than confessionalism to the creative process. One of the opening poems in that book, "360 Degrees of Detachment," claims that in nature, separation is more "ancient than knowledge," then proceeds to consider such phenomena as the earth splitting off from a stellar cloud, silt and pebbles breaking loose from rocks, as well as the intriguing fact that the calcium inside the bones of each of us is part of some scattered ancient star. But, unlike a severed marriage, nature's broken fibers of connection can rejoin,

> . . . knot together
> like newly dividing cells that join to make an eye,
> a fingerprint, a bone.

In another poem of that time I call myself "a connoisseur of small deaths / —zippers, curtains, shutting eyelids." Depression's black hand intrudes in a lament addressed to a broom with freakish hair, whose once "fluently carved" bark has hollowed to an empty red stick, "for witches to mount . . . impelled by pent-up lust." Blame it all on the deformed broom, but I bemoan my own lost "claims to sorcery" (my fading sense of omnipotence) for my inability to sweep away anything except the debris of everyday life, its dust and black lemon rinds. More desirable the power to make the broom truly sweep,

> as in wing, sail or soar; a great shawl of wind
> that will lift from my heart its lead case
> reshape it: a great Buddhist temple bell.

Despite the scientific content of many poems in this book, doubtless influenced by Dr. S.'s own interest in the sciences, that old black wish for easy magical solutions managed to resurface. Like therapy itself, the poems evolved, psychologically if not esthetically, in more of a spiraling than a linear fashion. Of course, the creative process itself works the same way, following a logic of its own rather than Socratic logic.

Likewise my obsession with the past, a dominant theme in *The Politics of Snow* (2001), though in that volume I try in two linked poems to transcend the obsession by a series of quasi-scientific, often wry, cause and effect statements on memory and forgetting. Elsewhere I touch upon one of my favorite images, the crystal, in an attempt to turn Villon upside down by asserting that less important than the snows of yesteryear are "the snows yet to come." Whether my optimism in these poems represents an effort to please Dr. S. with my progress, the prefiguration of a desired state of mind, or an actual, if temporary, conviction, is as mysterious as the urge to write poetry itself. Especially given these poems' ironic tone: Dr. S.'s major esthetic lapse was a lack of enthusiasm for irony and literary wit. Yet both before and during therapy, I use the voice of irony nearly as often as my more lyrical and meditative voices. (I usually did not bother to bring in such work, not wanting to risk a resurgence of damning with faint praise.)

The expansion of the creative process away from concerns with myself to both political and scientific issues continues to this day. My most recent book, *Photo, Bomb, Red Chair* (2004), takes its title from a poem inspired by an article about the loss of lives in the latest suicide bombing in an Israeli market; I am indeed present, but as an observer from far away, safe in the shiny suburban shopping mall where I began to write the poem. Loss and mourning can also stimulate creativity, though grief itself inhibits the process. At the same time as the Israeli poem, I was troubled by my elderly father's deteriorating health, yet I managed to go beyond my often contradictory feelings about his imminent death by making a general comment on the futility of very old people's dreams, reminding them that "The War's Long Over / All the Shops Have Closed for the Season." I recall not only the relief of openly expressing my ambivalence about my ailing father but also Dr. S.'s warm response to the poem. No more of that love/like pother, but a ratification of my work in general and the particular expression of a hitherto *verboten* wish that my much-loved but difficult father would finally let go and die. I'm sure I would not have written that poem had therapy not liberated me to express such disturbing thoughts.

Yet by no means do I claim that the interplay of poetry and therapy always proceeded smoothly, even after many years of treatment. One example involves a poem called "Fog Horns" and Dr. S.'s reactions, particularly his effort to add a new dimension to the poem (not to be confused with his occasional suggestions about a particular word or stanza break and other such technical matters). The poem itself, partly quoted below, is not one of my most important; my motive for presenting it to him was relatively simple: another poem to fill in the potential gaps of a therapy session, to forestall the silence I so feared. Indeed, I had established the habit of carrying at least two recent poems in my purse, my quasi-magical talismans to call upon when needed. Here's the final version of the poem; the italic lines show my incorporation of Dr. S.'s suggestions, offered not for technical but therapeutic reasons.

> Fog horns are frustrated opera stars.
> Instead of singing Wagner at the Met
> they spend their lives warning
> boats to slow down, avoid seawalls
>
> .   .   .   .
>
> *urging lonely old women and men*
> *to sing with them, both the long buried—*
> *responding to the music*
> *as the dead might do in dreams—*
> *and previews of myself . . .*

Originally I had noted in the second stanza only the words "lonely old men and women," imagining widows and widowers who live alone in their cottages along the coast of Maine. The words "previews of myself" as I age represented my identification with those imaginary people lying alone in bed after many days of risking loss of their voices because they had not spoken to anyone at all. Dr. S., however, linked those people to my own long-buried ancestors and, by implication, their continuing power over me—not exactly a new theme in my work. By appearing in dreams (as they often did), the dead ancestors reveal that they are still alive in my unconscious. I argued with Dr. S. that he was deliberately projecting an idea into the poem which would modify its intent; he responded by attributing my objection to my fear of those dead ancestors, but he also saw it as a sign of what Harold Bloom called "the anxiety of influence." If I changed the poem, would it no longer be mine, but a hybrid of his ideas and mine? In other words, would I be changing it to accommodate to him? Perhaps he was right in therapeutic terms, but would the poem suffer as a result? I argued some more but in the closing moments of the session began to incorporate his suggestion; as soon as I entered my car, I proceeded to lock the changes into place. The gain? Possibly a better, or at least a more interesting, poem. And the reopening of my longtime obsession with the past in a somewhat different context. The loss, real or imagined? Dr. S. had become the co-creator of my poem, thus threatening my narcissistic belief in my creative originality. Incorporating his suggestion could also be a sign of cowardice and my overidentification with Dr. S.

Co-creation in a therapeutic context, as distinguished from incorporation of helpful suggestions from friends or workshops, can be a difficult problem when poetry and therapy are closely intertwined: especially when I would compromise by incorporating his more benign interpretations of certain poems' underlying themes. Granted, such suggestions have often led to revisions that, in the process, improve the poem as a poem. Which, on a psychological level, raises again the problem of distinguishing between prefiguration, wishful thinking, and the genuinely felt. One recent example involves a poem about how the memory of a creek near my grandparents' summer house many decades ago interfered with my appreciation of a newly discovered creek, the reminder contaminating the present experience, as if this creek contained some toxic substance. After discussing the poem in a therapy session, I spontaneously revised it, making the "first creek" flow into all the other creeks I might experience, the remembered moment becoming part of a process beyond myself instead of an isolated memory, an expansion rather than a constriction. Such a view of the intertwining of past and present is considerably more salubrious than my longtime obsession with memories. But do I really and deeply believe the revised point of view? Or is it a prefiguration of a change yet to be embedded within, or, worse, merely wishful thinking? I suspect I won't know the answer for quite a while.

Another difficulty is my fear that my writing, especially of poetry, has become an addiction, which in turn intensifies the addictive nature of my long-term therapy, at the very least extending the therapy for fear that I will cease writing if I am no longer a patient. That old and, I dare say, universal fear of silence, the blank page or canvas. Still another danger involves a possible overestimation of the merits of my work, which intensifies my disappointment when others do not recognize my abilities as much as Dr. S. usually does. And there's also a potential confusion between a poem's literary and therapeutic merits, even though the poetry-therapy connection came about spontaneously: never did Dr. S. suggest poetry exercises in order to bring a conflict to the surface or control a conflict by pinning a smile button on sadness or pain.

Of course, not every poem I've written has therapeutic implications, whether shared or not. But overall, the integration of poetry and therapy has been, and continues to be, a definite plus in terms of clarifying feelings and ideas and, especially, expanding them, thus enhancing whatever talents I have. Certainly I have revised poems far more than in the past. Would I have written all those poems, stories, and so on, without Dr. S.'s encouragement and the implicit assurance of at least a one-person audience, despite my decent publishing record? Impossible question. Likewise the question of whether I will be able to dissociate my creative work from him. I end with a poem called "The Crystal," in which the crystal does not reveal the future; instead, glints from its imagined facets offer a potential resolution to my old obsession with the past.

Like that crystal, the poem's primary image suddenly arrived while I sat in a cafe near Rome's Piazza Navone. It

> bounces over the stones, bobs to rest
> at my feet, between the pigeons
> blown trash and bottles
>
> . . . .
>
> after a day when memories rained so hard
> no umbrella could deflect them.

I tap, then bang the crystal on the piazza's stones, a fantasy of retrieval of "at least a single lost second, even if/the globe shatters, a Pandora's box in disguise."

The last two stanzas express both confusion and fear, but culminate in a recognition of my ongoing life, given the hypothesized expansion of the crystal from within. When I try to destroy it, it resists the smallest fracture, bouncing above the poplars and landing at my feet. As evening falls, I leave the piazza, abandoning the crystal and asking of the air, "is the crystal complete / with no room for any more years?" But I cannot forget the crystal and what it contains of even the very recent past:

> Yet I keep walking, refuse to turn back,
> for surely its facets must have captured
> the few moments between
> the time I left the Piazza Navone
> and when that crystal
> first came to rest at my feet.

Going beyond the poem, let me say that the expanding crystal has likely captured the many moments between when I first started this essay and now type this sentence, just as it captures the fifty minutes of a therapeutic hour, expanding and self-creating until yet another session, yet another poem.

THOUGH I TOOK SEVERAL medications over the years, including antidepressants, I found no particular correlation between medication and creativity. At most, dexedrine, used for a time to potentiate the antidepressants—none of which worked very well—increased my energy enough to prolong the number of hours I could write, but it did not affect form or content or stimulate new ideas.

Thirteen

IN THE COUNTRY OF MOTHERHOOD

MARTHA SILANO, MFA

Giving birth is like waking up in a foreign country where you know neither the language nor the customs.

—DR. REX GENTRY

PLEASE HELP ME hold up the walls, I asked politely enough. They were beginning to tremble. No one moved. I yelled, "Help me!" A few of my compatriots came nervously forward, one even taking a place at the wall. "Here, hold this part right here!" But it was no use. The walls were really shaking now. Soon we would all be crushed. I looked out the window and saw a blinding white light in the sky. It was God. He had a message for me. He was tired, could I please take over for a little while? I said I would, but first I would have to find a way through these window bars.

Two male nurses tackled me and threw me onto my bed, strapping me in. I felt the prick of a needle.

My husband likes to brag that I can write anywhere, even at stoplights. But motherhood was unlike any red light I had ever come up against.

The first three weeks after giving birth, I was too wound up to sleep much, too worried to relax, insecure about every aspect of mothering. Giving my son a bath, I worried he'd catch pneumonia. When he cried, I blamed myself. My stomach ached with the anxiety of not being able to make him stop. A book of poems gathered dust on my nightstand, along with my writing journal.

My husband went out on an errand, leaving me at home alone with the baby. He started crying, so I reached for the Beatles songbook—every kid likes the Beatles, right? I tried singing, rocking, nursing, and more singing, but nothing helped. "Bang, bang, Maxwell's silver hammer came down upon his head," I nearly screamed. I called my midwife. "Do you think you might hurt your baby?" she asked. "I don't want to be left alone with him."

Red and blue lights flashed down our block. I was standing on the threshold of the front door, not in and not out of the house. The police brushed past me. In the nursery they found my infant son lying in a bassinette, calm and quiet. They carried him into the squad car and took him to the hospital where I'd given birth. By then the midwife and my husband had both arrived. We drove to the hospital to figure out what was wrong with me.

I looked through my diary for clues. There were plenty:

Read half a poem today, a little of the *New York Times*. Other than that, ate, slept, nursed, nursed, nursed.

Haven't had a free moment to write till now, though time to nurse, sleep, eat, nurse, sleep, eat.

In a day I accomplish so little—never did find the time to tie my hair in a pony tail.

I left the hospital with a prescription for sleep medication. But a few days later I started slipping in and out of reality. My husband knew something was seriously wrong when I wrapped myself in a blanket like a funeral pall and apologized for leaving him alone with our newborn. "Now I understand," I explained. "I'm dead." Convinced my milk was poison, I refused to nurse.

He had my mother on the next flight to Seattle. By morning I was catatonic, lying on my back and staring at the ceiling, unable to speak, unable to even blink. At Harborview Medical Center, where I was involuntarily admitted by county mental health officials, I was diagnosed with postpartum psychosis. Five years later, I wrote "Harborview."

. . . some god's gotten hold of me,
some god's squeezed hard the spit-up rag of my soul

. . . .

some god's got me thinking my milk's poison, unfit
for a hungry child, some god's got me pacing

. . . .

doesn't want me well, doesn't want my rapid-fire brain
to slow, wants this ride for as long as it lasts, wants to take it

to its over-Niagara-in-a-barrel end, which is where
this god is taking me, one rung at a time, one ambulance,

one EMT strapping me in, throwing me off this earth
. . . .
Some god till I'm believing I've been shot, guts dribbling out,

till I'm sure . . . I'm dead, a ghost, a smoldering corpse.

Harborview (including one week in the ICU locked ward) was my home for the better part of a month. There I received heavy doses of Risperdal (antipsychotic medication), Ativan (antianxiety medication), Klonopin (antianxiety medication), and Celexa (antidepressant medication). The latent Catholicism of my Polish-Italian heritage visited me in the form of waking visions. I saw God, and angels battled devils for my attention. Strangely, I was also visited by the Unabomber, and at one point I was convinced I had the power to destroy the world with the push of a button. The hallucinations tapered off after a week of heavy sedation, replaced by a gloomy, zombielike state. By the time of my discharge, I no longer suffered from delusions, but I was still extremely paranoid, often thinking that the nurses, patients, and hospital staff were talking about me. I assumed I would be mentally ill for the rest of my life. For months I moved around the house as if trying to swim through mud, unable to say more than a few words at a time.

I'd been warned that I might suffer from bouts of depression, that my recovery would be long and slow. I hadn't expected to be suicidal. I didn't have "a plan," but one day while strolling my baby along a lake near our home, I considered filling my pockets with stones, like Virginia Woolf, and walking in. Sometimes I thought of drowning us both. A few years later I wrote:

AT THE SAYRES PARK ROWING AND SAILING CENTER,
LAKE WASHINGTON, SEATTLE

This is the body of water I once considered
slipping into . . .
. . . .
                                    . . . These are the gulls
that preened, pecked, molted to brilliant white
all without my notice. This is the body of water

I planned, like the bread that ducks can't always catch,
to sink into.

This fuguelike state, though not as acutely painful as psychosis, tested my will. I had difficulty believing I would recover. Somewhere beneath all the layers of confusion I knew I had been a writer once. Reading what I'd written the summer before both surprised and saddened me. Pregnancy had been a prolific time. I'd written "Getting Kicked by a Fetus" and "What They Don't Tell You about the Ninth Month," lively and musical poems. My inability to write only exacerbated the depression. I mourned my past life as a poet, fully believing I would never put pen to paper again. I used to be a poet, I thought to myself, now I'm a mom. Friends and relatives told me that of course I would write again, that my condition was temporary, but I didn't believe them.

The first post-psychosis doctor prescribed megadoses of Neurontin, which turned out, famously, to be a placebo marketed by a feckless pharmaceutical company. The second listened to my story and mused, "Sounds like Persephone." Seventy-five dollars, please. Doctor #3 worked on getting me to realize I loved my son. If we could do that, I would be healed. Then I began hearing about another doctor, named Rex Gentry. Unlike the others, he was a psychiatrist specializing in postpartum cases. Why were there so few?

I went to hear him speak. Unassuming and soft-spoken, Dr. Gentry explained what happens to new mothers. First of all, their senses are more acute (an adaptive strategy to increase the chances of an infant's survival). Also, they're hardwired to protect their infants, causing the rapid and steady release of adrenaline. This adrenalin release, he explained, often leads to sleeplessness and a greater risk of anxiety attacks. There were medicines to slow down this release, and there were also ways to keep a new mom from slipping into depression. When I presented myself to this man after his talk, he must've seen the half-crazed look in my eye. "Call my secretary," he said, "and make sure she gives you an appointment."

Dr. Gentry approached the postpartum period from both a psychological and a physiological standpoint. New moms were bound to feel out of sorts, and I was one of them. It wasn't surprising or shocking. I'd simply woken up in a foreign country without a map, without a dictionary, with no way to understand this strange place. This, he explained, was probably why non-Western cultures pampered and protected new mothers in the calm and quiet of their homes during the first month after giving birth. While "doing the month," he explained, female friends and midwives assisted the new mother with household tasks, ensuring social seclusion and a mandated rest period, recognizing her vulnerability and state of transition into the motherhood role.

While new moms in other lands were surrounded by their grand-moms, mommies, a whole cache of aunties, here in the good ol' US of A my husband and I had foolishly made a pact to go it alone—no familial interference for us. Okay, so we were clueless.

Not only had I been going it without my female posse, but I was also feeling tremendous pressure to rise to the ridiculous expectations Western societies place on new mothers—and quickly realizing I couldn't pull it off. I was no June Cleaver. I wasn't even Mrs. Brady. And while I'd listened carefully (had even taken notes) about the baby blues and the risk for more serious depression, when I started in with the all-day crying jags, barely able to dress myself let alone write a sentence, nobody—least of all me—knew quite what to do.

But Dr. Gentry didn't stigmatize or judge me. Instead, he normalized my experience: it was what all women went through, more or less. Looking back, I'm nearly certain that my own body chemistry, including a rapid decline in estrogen production, spurred on my psychotic episode, not the missing gang-o-gals. But in order to get well it was crucial to downplay what set me apart from the other 999 new moms. What I needed was a sense of belonging. If psychosis had been my fifteen minutes of fame, the rest of my reactions to new motherhood had to be ordinary. Mundanely usual. The Norm.

As we continued to work together, Rex established what a new mom *must have* during the months after giving birth. First of all, she needed plenty of sleep—two four-hour blocks a night. Another was time for herself, at least one hour a day. She might also need medicines to diminish her overalertness. This all made perfect sense to me, but I still had some residual phobias from the psychosis. One was a fear of being alone in the house. When I told Rex about this, he assured me it was a totally reasonable reaction: "someone might break in, right?" Exactly. Then he reminded me of the likelihood of a break-in. "Odds are, not a chance." Reasonable enough, I decided, and slowly my fear began to fade.

Rex (everyone calls him Rex) often operated this way. Something would be bugging me, and he would provide a solution that actually worked. Take, for instance, my fear of flying. He began by telling me about one of his patients, an executive at Microsoft. "Got all the way to the airport once. Bought his ticket. Stood in line to board. Panicked. Turned around and went home. A powerful man, but he can't get on a plane." Establishing that average, sane people experience unexplainable fears was crucial for me. That advice and a prescription for Xanax (antianxiety medication) were all it took.

Rex emanated understanding. His wife had suffered from severe postpartum mood disorder after the birth of their first child, so he'd been through it. It didn't fluster him that I'd lived through a complete break with reality. "Psychosis is just a series of waking nightmares," he said, "nightmares you believe are true." When he told me this, I began to think differently: my psychosis wasn't really all that terrible—it was just an extreme reaction to what all new mothers face after giving birth.

All this was helping, but Rex still had serious work to do. Basically, the hospital had put together the wrong cocktail of medications. He needed to wean me off selective serotonin reuptake inhibitors (SSRIs) and introduce lithium and Depakote, which are used to treat symptoms of bipolar disorder. Within a month or two of this switch, I started to feel better. Amazingly, I felt the urge to write. Soon I was sitting at the computer, focusing long enough to take notes for a poem. The first poem I completed, "Song for a Newborn," let loose the elation and wonder I was finally able to express for our now five-month-old son:

> Oh my Double Thick Pork Chop,
> my Prawn Tequila-kissed,
> Most Pico of Pico de Gallos:
> bless your brain . . . your capillaries
> like the roots of Early Girls,
> your large intestine like dozens
> of miniature knackwursts.
> Bless your liver, its 500 functions.
> Bless your sternum, your scapula—
> heck: bless all your 206 bones.

Strange, you might say, that what poured out of me first was so positive, but I had no interest in writing about psychosis. I was feeling good enough to smile and laugh, and smile and laugh was what I wanted to do.

I was also learning that naptime was not only important for babies. Another poem from this time, "While He Naps," begins:

> Like tulips wrapped in cellophane, a nap is a beautiful thing.
> Like the wind before it starts to rain, a nap is beautiful
> like a lawn near a lake where you lay yourself down.

Naptime quickly became my writing time. Wherever we were headed—grocery store, park, gym—I carried a notebook. When he fell asleep in his car seat—voilà!—out came my pen and notebook. It took a little while to figure out, but I was beginning to get it: write when you can, not according to a schedule. Let go of having a quiet place. Your office is your car, a blanket at the park, even the stationary bike at the YMCA. Before long, I was in a groove, writing poems about my son's first attempts at speech, then the questions he asked over and over, and then how it felt to send him off to preschool. I was unstoppable; I'd found my niche, my raison d'être.

I remained on lithium and Depakote for almost two years. When the danger of relapsing passed, I went off all medications except the occasional dose of Klonopin for sleep. I saw Rex for what I thought would be my final visit in early 2004. Soon after I found myself pregnant.

Our second child was born in early 2005. Gone were the deep-seated insecurities about mothering, but despite my confidence I began having symptoms—racing thoughts, manic-like elation, paranoia, fears about where my children were and if they were okay—soon after giving birth. This time, however, we were ready with the right medication, immediately. Instead of letting elation turn to full-blown mania, I had Zyprexa, a sedating atypical antipsychotic medication that is also used to treat manic symptoms. I was able to write during my daughter's first months of life, including a poem about her birth:

I CAN'T WRITE

about her birth . . .

.   .   .   .
           . . . or the number of times I pushed,
but I can tell you [about] the voices of children,

of mothers telling them to settle down, how I wished my womb,
like theirs, had returned to the size of a fist. And I can tell you

I wished my daughter were older than half a day . . . both of us
smelling not only of yeast but of the acrid, earthiness of colostrum,

of colostrum and vernix and blood.

After what I'd experienced with my first child, it still seems miraculous to me that I was able to write poems shortly after giving birth. Motherhood was no longer a foreign place, so I didn't panic when I occasionally had to choose between naptime and writing time. When I snuck in a few hours to write, I was focused, imaginative, original— at my best. As with my first child, what came most naturally was exuberance.

IN THE COUNTRY OF MOTHERHOOD

In the month of pastels, fluorescent pink grass

. . . .

With wheat berry eyebrows, resides

in the batter of Proust's madeline.
Of cantaloupe rind, of gargantuan zucchini.

Of Athena—all brains from the get-go, over-
brimming, teeming, full of knowing

hare-bell from bluebell, every genus
and every species, all brushed up

on conifer know-how, reminding us
spruces have papery cones.

Of granite, with meteor shower
skin, her nose, when it sniffs,

pre- and just- rainfall . . . She's
the Thinker, Ye Olde Tick Tock.

She's the patch of geraniums
in full throttle, all wrists and sucking fists.

She's what glows and glows.

Unlike in "Song for a Newborn," however, in this poem I'd moved from writing specifically about my child to writing about all girls. The therapeutic relationship with Rex had helped me create poetry that reaches beyond not only my own insecurities and fears but even my own children. Now I was writing poems with a more universal, all-encompassing vision.

In her book *Mother Shock: Loving Every (Other) Minute of It,* Andrea J. Buchanan outlines the stages of culture shock for the purpose of showing how new mothers share a similar bout with the new and frightening world of motherhood. From an initial honeymoon phase to a feeling of being cut off completely from cultural cues, new moms only very slowly begin to see themselves as mothers. As a poet, I had to learn that having a child would not prevent me from being creative. This was not an instinctive process. Over the months and years since giving birth, children have become my most popular subject. Looking toward my children for inspiration, I find the well is deep; indeed, it is bottomless.

Fourteen

DOWN THE TRACKS

BRUCE SPRINGSTEEN SANG TO ME

LIZA PORTER

Upstairs a band was playin', the singer was singin' something about goin' home. —BRUCE SPRINGSTEEN

NINETEEN SEVENTY-EIGHT, twenty-one years old, five years out of high school, just divorced for the first time, I'm sitting in my '69 Camaro, a girl car—white with cracked vinyl top and a dented back bumper, two-door, three-speed, 250 cubic inches—the one thing of material value I got out of my violent first marriage. I drive past the university and south onto the freeway in Eugene, Oregon. It's raining, always raining.

Bruce Springsteen blasting on the 8-track about *streets of fire* and *badlands* and *darkness on the edge of town*. I'm way too skinny, wearing a stretchy green-and-white striped halter-top, no bra, men's Levi corduroys cut all the way up to the top of my thighs. Long blonde hair flying out the window, back into my blue eyes, into my mouth and out again. Kool in my left hand, fingers of my right tapping the steering wheel to the beat of Springsteen's *The Promised Land*.

A couple of months later, or a day, or a week, sitting in my stifling studio apartment on Olive Street, battleship-gray steel-and-cement-beamed high-rise; piles of clothes on the floor in front of a full-length mirror, can't decide what to wear, give up, sit on the edge of the couch, a huge whale-shaped ceramic ashtray full of butts in front of me, pick out the longest one and light it up, can't possibly leave the apartment to go buy a pack, stuck my finger down my throat twice last night after stuffing myself with ice cream and granola, couldn't shit this morning, how will I ever get to work?

I open my carved-wood East Indian box with the hinged lid, take out the Zig-Zags and roll a joint. I'll just get paranoid smoking alone, but what else can I do but get high? I need to change how I feel. Pile Springsteen's first four albums on the turntable, drop the needle. Something about "madmen drummers, bummers and Indians in the summer."[1] Flick my lighter, light the joint. Ah, there we go. The stories. The voice. The guitar. The smoke. Some kind of hope.

A WEEK OR SO AGO, Vonnie, my best friend from high school—perhaps my only friend, I see now—contacted me through the Internet. During the three decades since we last talked, sometimes I ached for her like a child for its mother, felt as if parts of me had been stolen when we lost touch, and I'd never recovered those pieces. After we e-mailed back and forth a few times and arranged to meet, I began thinking about how each of us had been desperately searching for something back then—a way to speak our truth, maybe a way to speak at all. Adrift in a world of stressed-out families and war and overcrowded schools, we'd been each other's voices: the ones we tried out our ideas on, told our secrets to, got unconditional acceptance from. It wasn't until I started writing twenty years after high school that I realized what I'd lost.

I thought about the huge part music played in our lives back then. Like most of our generation, we had a soundtrack for our dramas— Carole King, Elton John, Neil Young, Joan Baez, Simon and Garfunkel, the Moody Blues. A cacophony of voices—some quiet as poetry, others louder than God. In junior high and high school, Vonnie and I sat for hours on my living room floor listening to albums, reading the liner notes, so self-absorbed, searching for clues, for a "key to the universe," as Springsteen sings in *Growin' Up,* but whereas his answer was in "the engine of an old parked car,"[2] ours was hidden in the words of all the great song travelers, the first voices I'd ever wanted to make my own. They told their truths with beauty and music. I didn't yet know what my truths were. I think I needed to get to the roots of my anger and learn to voice it.

During the drive to Phoenix to visit Vonnie, I played old Springsteen cassettes—*Darkness on the Edge of Town, Born to Run, The River*—reliving my youth, on the road, listening to Springsteen's voice reaching for the Promised Land. Vonnie and I talked for hours. I told her about the depression I've struggled with most of my life, how I always thought it was my fault that I couldn't find some sort of happiness. No matter how I tried to prove myself: perfect grades, competitive swimming, piano, flute, church choir, concert band—none of it relieved my depression.

"I remember you being angry, so very angry," she said, looking straight at me. "Hell, *I* was angry." We laughed, the crinkles of age and hard-earned wisdom forming parentheses around our eyes.

I *was* angry. At the fucked-up world, at how numb I felt all the time, at how nothing I did seemed to change anything. I could barely open my mouth at all, let alone ask for help. My starkest memory of my teenage years is silence—around me, in me, a dark silence that nothing could penetrate.

I always searched outside myself for something to fight the depression inside me—a place of twisted mouths yelling, ridiculing, trying to destroy me every waking minute, even in my dreams. I had nothing to fight back with. So I gave up trying. I started using drugs and alcohol to shut up those destructive voices. Though my silence was lonely and desolate, it was better than those taunts I'd accepted into my soul that convinced me I was worthless.

Just before Vonnie got hold of me, I'd come out of another months-long depression after two wonderful years of remission. Those nasty voices grew roots inside me again. Partly the result of my sister's death earlier in the year, this episode took me deeper into that dark silence than I'd been in a long, long time.

I'm convinced anyone who has a voice—is born with it and learns to exercise it as he or she grows to adulthood—never even thinks about it.

This is where my path to becoming a writer begins. My path through depression. The crooked journey to find my voice.

AFTER I LEAVE my first husband and start living on my own for the first time, Springsteen's songs become the soundtrack of my life. Because I'm so lost, because I have so little control over my own life, I live in his stories—so much better than my own. The characters living on those first four albums—Wendy and Mary and Wild Billy and Crazy Janey and Spanish Johnny—are my friends. The music works as a sort of antidepressant—a mind-altering substance kicking in my adrenalin and keeping me alive or at least able to drag myself through the world until something different happens. Instead of focusing on my failures, I enter into Springsteen's sad and angry songs about fast cars and darkness, dead-eyed girls hanging out on porches at dusk in desolate areas of town. I project all of my anger into those songs. The lyrics are my mantras, soothing me and accepting me into another world. Springsteen and his friends sit with me in the front seat of my Camaro, teaching me how to speak. I listen to his music so much, like a true fanatic I even start calling him Bruce. His songs become secret voices in my head that I vow no one will ever take away from me.

A few years after getting divorced, I enroll in a community college. I don't really know what a poem is, but I take my first poetry class. My first poem:

IN SYNC

the moon's light
is it her child
or does she live in hope
every month
at the movement of my womb
when she's her fullest?

does she wish she had
a source of her own
instead of reflecting
another's power?

Powerlessness. Absence of voice. I'd given my power to my family, my husband, and my unexpressed anger, and then to drinking, drugging, destroying myself with bulimia, anorexia, compulsive exercising, dangerous men.

I'm seeing a therapist for the first time. She has the same name as the main character in Bruce's *Fourth of July, Asbury Park* (Sandy). A confessor more than a path out of my desperation, Sandy keeps me alive with her acceptance and kind attempts to help me. She insists I join her women's group (to get me out of my isolation, I'm sure). I am silent the whole sixteen weeks. The women are nice, but I'm petrified to open my mouth.

At one point, I can't leave my apartment. Sandy sends me to an MD who prescribes Elavil. It kicks me in the butt and gets me moving again—back to school and work—but eventually the side effects ("hangover" mornings, strange visions) are too much, and I quit the medication and turn back to my friend, the booze.

An excerpt from another poem I wrote then:

I cried for everyone tonight
for myself . . .
for the way my friend had to drive me around
after I drank to the rain
. . . my tears the downpour

LIZA PORTER

the puddle in the laundromat parking lot, floating
Marlboros smoked down beyond the filter
. . . .
and I know
I KNOW
what it's like to scrape bottom

I really *want* to write, but I can't sit still long enough. I'm anxious all the time. I can't channel it into the energy to create a poem—or into anything. I have to drink a bottle of wine every night to get to sleep. I can't cry, I can't get angry, I am dead inside. Writing poetry doesn't help. It brings up things I don't want to deal with. I drop out of the poetry class halfway through the semester and then out of school altogether. I've failed again. Something is wrong with me, I can't figure it out. I'm convinced it's my fault, and I possess no voice to ask for the right kind of help. I dive into the booze and drugs and barely survive the next few years.

Depression steals the voice. Silence breeds depression. Depression breeds silence.

NINETEEN EIGHTY, twenty-four years old, I "escape" from Oregon and follow my sister to Arizona. Thirteen hundred miles on the road— Bruce singing to me from his newest album, *The River.* I play it over and over, I sing every lyric, memorize every word, whine when Bruce whines, wail when Bruce wails, speeding down that highway, celebrating the worst and best of his characters' lives. My favorite song is *Drive All Night,* of course; my favorite line, corny as it is: "I swear I'd drive all night again just to buy you some shoes."[3]

Somewhere deep inside me lives a glimmer of hope—a bright sun shining on an icy river as spring comes to the forest. "We'd go down to the river and into the river we'd dive, oh down to the river we'd ride."[4] Poetry. A river of redemption, almost a baptism, being born again after years of craving and crashing. Possibility. This is what I hope I'll find in Arizona. The desert. Rebirth. The Promised Land.

DURING THE FIRST YEAR in Arizona, I found sobriety, married for the second time, and gave birth to my first child. I traded Bruce's voice for the voices around the twelve-step tables, and one voice in particular—that of the man I married. I traded Bruce's voice of struggle and faith for the overbearing voice of this mean, critical man. I didn't speak once during a twelve-step meeting the first two years of sobriety; I just sat and listened. I was still so silenced by the depression and my husband that his words became the *word*; his voice, the *voice*. He forbade listening to rock music—said it was from the Devil. I stayed with him until three months after our daughter was born. Without music, without voice, my purpose in my life was to care for our daughter.

During the first three months of her life, I became a different person. Staying sober and nurturing my daughter—feeding her from my body, comforting her when she cried, keeping up with the dirty diapers—were the first accomplishments I'd managed in many years.

An excerpt from a poem written later about my experience:

Trust me, I know every single word of that old Dylan song

. . . stumbling down small town streets . . . our child the bundle of kindling to restart the almost dead spark in me, . . . boulders in Beaver Creek rolled and knocked . . . that violent cracking all night long . . . We're losers, we're rolling stones, you yelled at me when we got out boxes the eighth time that year, as if blaming someone would change it.

My voice became an advocate for my daughter. Finally, I had something to live for, someone to take care of because I couldn't do that for myself, didn't think I was worth it. When my husband criticized my mothering skills one more time ("Shouldn't the baby have a sweater on?"), that was *it*. I was done. I took my daughter and a suitcase full of cloth diapers and got on a Greyhound bus headed south to live with my sister until I figured out what to do next. I was determined to raise my daughter in a home free of harsh criticism and shame.

On welfare, then working low-paying clerical jobs, I became spokesperson for my daughter, who had no voice yet, and this (and staying clean and sober) kept me alive, kept the depression at bay while I stubbornly persevered and learned to live sober in the world, worked the steps, got back into therapy, and concentrated on raising my daughter.

Here is the first stanza of a poem written and published years later, after treatment for depression, after my voice had grown to its strongest, when I was learning to turn my difficult experiences into something more than accusation or self-pity:

FIRST BORN

When she woke crying in the night
I'd lift her out of the crib

LIZA PORTER

and hold on for dear life. Hers, mine, the whole world's,
the darkness of the stone cabin
filled with the breath of all the other mothers
I knew held their babies
in the same way in the night's silence—
heads on the crook of our arms, tiny mouths
sucking at our breasts, new eyes glowing hunger fire,
all of us exhausted from the birthing
days or months before, all of us feeding
the bodies of the innocents, all of us madonnas.

Bruce's voice and his stories were still inside me, but now I was the
girl on *The River* wandering alone with my baby in a stroller, struggling
to get by. I actually pictured myself that way: walking through dark
streets to the tune of one of his songs—"Right between the eyes, baby,
point blank."[5] I was still a victim, still depressed and angry, of course,
but Bruce was still singing in my ear. No matter how bad things were,
I still searched for hope, faith, the Promised Land.

FIVE YEARS LATER, I remarried, gave birth to a second daughter, and
settled down to "live happily ever after." I'd never known I wanted a
family until I had one. I wanted to love and be loved like anyone else,
and the safety I felt within this household made it possible for me to
start writing again. When both girls were school age, I enrolled in a
nighttime creative nonfiction class at the local community college and
began writing the only stories I knew—my struggles and failures up to
that point in my life. Thirty-eight years old, sober for fourteen years, I
wrote about my addictions, my childhood, my first two marriages, the
doctor who had molested me when I was sixteen, the time I was date-
raped. The safety of my family made it possible for me to tell the stories
I'd always kept secret. Because I was using my voice, the depression
stayed distant and silent for almost ten years.

Voice comes from safety. Silence becomes words. The truth can be
told.

Ah, but the *streets of fire* reappeared. The act of writing and the class
itself became a form of therapy for me. I took my stories in for cri-
tiquing, my skin so thin I wept in the car on the way home. I got angry
at my classmates' sometimes thoughtless remarks. But I refused to
quit. I used my anger to keep writing. A loud "I'll show them" (show
my classmates, my parents, my ex-husbands, the rapist, the world?)
echoed inside me, driven by the process of writing and a desperate

need to be heard. On the front page of one essay titled "Mugshot," my teacher wrote "You have found your voice. *The Voice.*" I wasn't quite sure what he meant, but it made me feel strong and powerful. An excerpt from "Mugshot":

I can't believe it fucking fifteen years since I seen your face & all of a sudden it flashes in my mind just one eerie frame from an early DeNiro film but it's your face fills that space . . . your contempt for the world arcing out like sparks off the chains of a Fifties' street gang, heavy steel swinging & hitting the midnight . . . my eyes track the rage in those black eyes, my whole being waits it's only a matter of time my body braced like a stone fortress my teeth clenched—just like yours. Ready. Waiting. I want it I deserve it I crave it I pushed you toward it many times. I hate myself for that.

It took many years for me to accept this loud, harsh, baiting, biting, writing voice. While writing "Mugshot," I felt a fist pushing around inside me, down through my mouth, my stomach, my intestines, this trail of words moving so violently inside me I felt sick, as if a strangled voice were writhing around inside my body, a snake trying to escape. I fought this voice, its gracelessness, its raw flinging of angry words onto the page. But I couldn't stop it. It was mine. If I wanted to keep writing, I had to accept it.

For so long, I'd listened to the depression, I wasn't aware of any other voices inside me except the nasty critical ones, let alone this loud one and the challenge it presented, not just to me, but to others. My teacher reassured me that our writing is never as loud to others as it is to us. "And besides," he said, "I think you secretly *like* that voice. And besides that, there's nothing you can do about it."

EARLY 1998, age forty-two, four years writing—I hear the poet Quincy Troupe read at a book festival in Flagstaff. Along with the words in his poems, the way he uses his voice and body impresses me. Dreadlocks flying, hips swinging, hands waving, he is a musical instrument. Words and music transforming harsh stories into beautiful images and sounds. Like Bruce.

At the same festival, I sit in the audience while Joy Harjo recites her poems and plays saxophone with her band, Poetic Justice. Again, it isn't the words that affect me so much, but here is someone—a woman, for Christ's sake—up on a stage sharing her work, her music, her stories. Using her God-given voice! Her performance speaks to me the way Bruce's albums did when I piled them on the turntable twenty-some years before. Watch out poetry, here I come!

I'd written a few poems before that experience in Flagstaff. In my first poetry workshop, from an exercise prompt, this poem came through me:

SISTER

Sometimes when I think of O'Keeffe
I see rusty orange petals
and myself at twelve
going to you in the night
when the blood came.

My hands shaking, my face pink, I read the poem aloud to the people in the workshop, and a collective gasp rose from the table. I allowed this gasp—this appreciation of words that came out of me—to become mine. I thought: I can be a poet. I have things to say. I know what they are. I will use my voice.

I began going to an open microphone at a monthly reading series called the Lamplight. Putting my name on the sign-up sheet was almost scarier than actually going up in front of the audience to read. But I did it. I was petrified, almost shit in my pants the first few times, but something compelled me to do this thing that I'd seen Quincy Troupe and Joy Harjo and others do.

An excerpt from a poem written during that time:

THE RAPIST'S TALE

She could never come, not until she was 31
never give it up, no foot to the floor echoes
of celestial hymns, no strobe lights
at tunnel's end, no, only hard-won patient
waiting, someone else's waves spending
all her flesh and crashing onto bloody rocks.

I had to tell my stories. Like Bruce did, and still does. When I first read my poems out loud, I could hardly look up from my poems, ashamed to make eye contact, afraid my biggest fear would be fulfilled: I'd be punished for speaking out. Or someone would walk up to me after the reading and say: "Liar!" That abusive depression voice beating on me again—like someone trying to stomp on the coals in a fire pit to make sure not one spark is still burning.

My spark refused to go out—no matter how harsh my inner voice was or how much I worried about others' opinions. The things I write about are not pretty or comforting, never have been, and probably never will be. I think I've written two humorous poems in my life. Each new piece I write brings up another issue, another memory, something else I have to deal with, whether through therapy or the twelve steps. Or writing.

FEBRUARY 2001, forty-five years old, twenty years sober, seven years writing—after several years of scribbling morning pages at 5 AM before getting ready for work, revising poems during my lunch hours at the law firm, and on weekends at the mall while my daughters shop with their friends—the depression's back. It creeps up on me: the symptoms never show all at once, they sneak up until there are enough of them to get your attention (if you're lucky), or someone in your life notices something is terribly wrong and tells you. Personal problems get blown out of proportion. I run into furniture and door jambs, I can't concentrate, I'm edgy and worried, I cry all the time, I wake up in the middle of the night almost every night, I'm always exhausted, the hopelessness seeps its way back into my cells. For months, I limp in and out of depression, nothing going for me except my pathetic tenacity, trying my hardest to keep up with work, my husband, my kids, writing. I get scared.

Depression steals the voice. Silence breeds depression. Depression breeds silence.

DEATH CHANT

To weep, to shudder with the
dull, impossible gem
of grief, to freeze and never
move, to shout, to run
and keep running, to slap
God's face, to flap
heaving wings above it all, . . .

. . . .
. . . there it is, you, your
red howling rage.

LIZA PORTER

I call a psychiatrist recommended by my therapist. Dr. Garland sends me pages and pages of questions to complete before my first appointment. When we meet, he leans closer, with the papers in his hand. He has kind, twinkly eyes and wears a necklace of turquoise, and he says: "You've been clinically depressed most of your life and have never been properly treated for it." My shame dissipates a little. He explains brain chemistry, dopamine, serotonin reuptake inhibitors. He says, "I'll be able to help you. You may not feel better right away, and we might have to try many different medications, but I'll help you."

I raise my head and stare at him. I weep. And I believe him. I can't believe I believe him, but I do. Finally, I admit powerlessness. This is the first time I ever truly realize that it is not my fault; there is nothing more I can possibly do to fight the depression; all the running I've done, all my attempts to achieve things to prove I'm worthy, all the self-blame, none of it will work. I have an actual physical disease (like alcoholism), and there is treatment for it. I quit trying to convince myself that I have to fix it, or even that I *can* fix it. I decide to trust this doctor to help me find the right medication. Hope is back.

It takes almost three years to find the right combination of drugs to stabilize me. We go through Wellbutrin, Celexa, Effexor, Zoloft, Ritalin, Lamictal, Provigil, and Seroquel. More drugs I can't remember the names of, but I do recall the side effects—Zoloft gave me the shits, Effexor had me jerking and twitching in the night, Lamictal constipated me. I had to drink Senna tea every night so my bowels would move. Almost all of the drugs steal my sex drive. But something starts happening in my brain, I feel better, I begin to have faith in the process.

Some of the drugs work for a while and then suddenly stop; we try a new drug or a combination of drugs. I'm so discouraged, I tell Dr. Garland I want to quit. He encourages me at every appointment. He says, "You have a treatment-resistant depression, but we'll get it right. It might take a while." Again, I believe him.

The depression and its voices begin to recede into the background. I become able to write poems about things other than my sordid past, or with a more benevolent take on that past. After taking Wellbutrin and Lamictal for a while (which turn out to be the combination that works, along with a little Ritalin), I begin to write poems with more hope in them, beauty in images, in language; still angry, still trying to work things out inside me, but the poems become more accessible to others. Using the same material, my tempered voice tells the stories from a different, lighter place, but with the same "punch":

Praise to my big brother, who while nursing his hidden wounds
turned a refrigerator box into a rocket ship.
Praise his kind heart and quick mind, his meticulous design
of the windows, the control knobs, the dashboard
the gadgets he had no words for, but were surely needed
to survive with no gravity, no air.
Praise him for spending days in our garage staring
into the long hot summer and making this contraption
with his bare hands and naked soul. For not giving up.
Praise him for not giving up.

This is when my writing begins to change into art. My creative process, and therefore my voice, matures, assisted by my changed brain chemistry. I learn to wait in the silence instead of fighting it—to experience it as friend instead of enemy. I gain the focus and follow-through to discover the exact words and images to express what I want to say. This comes with experience as a writer—the more you write, the more you read, the more you learn—and I also attribute my increase in sensibility to medication, which makes me less driven, more willing to wait. The opposite of instant gratification, that horrible need to feel better, always to feel better and feel it *now*—the bane of addicts and depressives everywhere. My earlier writing had only helped me deal with my feelings and sort out my past. After the antidepressants begin to work, my work becomes more universal. Others besides me can relate to it. I have energy to submit poems to magazines. Editors begin accepting them. I learn—as a writer friend has told me several times—to turn the hardships of my life into beauty.

A poem published last year:

TRAINS

for Edie

This early in the morning the clouds have cleared
and I hear the whistles of train after train
rolling across the desert five miles south in the dark.

I remember trains, the one that carried you north
to the forest in autumn as if no other mode of travel
was good enough. But we had our own, didn't we,

the warm tongue of dope, cool teeth of booze
the dirty fingers of men whose names we could
never remember no matter how hard we tried.

What was it about us we hated so much?
Sleeping in strangers' beds was easier than even
approaching that age-old question. The ratty motor lodge

just south of Newport that summer, its depression-ware
dishes in dull primary colors, the muddy spring
trickling down to the beach like blood from a cut.

No one could ever sweep all the grit off those
chipped linoleum tiles. The two brothers who owned the place,
what did the older one's hands feel like on your skin?

I met a man just after you left, when we slid away
from the bar and headed out to his house
he was the nicest guy I'd ever known in my life.

But there were Nam-ghosts inside those walls, shadows
of his petrified wife and kids, he had to take a shower
just after we did it on the living room floor.

He laid a blanket down first and quoted Genesis to me.
The tracks were just behind his back fence and I could see myself
running along those shrieking metal rails

nothing but the clothes on my back and a photo
of you in my pocket, your scared eyes staring
at nothing. I pulled myself up into one of those empty cars

heading east or west, it didn't make any difference.
After I caught my breath, I glanced back toward town.
Not a single soul was watching.

Vonnie and I talk for six hours straight, as if we've been across-the-street neighbors our whole lives. Near the end of our visit, as we stand in her back yard, looking out toward the open desert, she says: "Remember how worried we always used to be about our weight?" Always binging or starving. Hating ourselves. I think of the time we found a twenty-dollar bill alongside the road and bought enough cookies and ice cream to stuff ourselves silly, how all that sugar lifted my depression, made me feel so high, only to crash back down a few hours later. I cringe at the thought.

BRUCE SPRINGSTEEN SANG TO ME

"Yeah," I say, rolling my eyes. "Sometimes I think about all that time I wasted worrying, I could've written ten novels or something." She looks at me with the same stunning eyes she had when we were fifteen. "Yeah. Or we could've been happy."

NOTES

Epigraph: "Incident on 57th Street," by Bruce Springsteen. Copyright © 1974 Bruce Springsteen, renewed 2002 © Bruce Springsteen (ASCAP). Reprinted by permission. International copyright secured. All rights reserved.

1. "Blinded by the Light," by Bruce Springsteen. Copyright © 1972 Bruce Springsteen, renewed 2000 © Bruce Springsteen (ASCAP). Reprinted by permission. International copyright secured. All rights reserved.

2. "Growin' Up," by Bruce Springsteen. Copyright © 1972 Bruce Springsteen, renewed 2000 © Bruce Springsteen (ASCAP). Reprinted by permission. International copyright secured. All rights reserved.

3. "Drive All Night," by Bruce Springsteen. Copyright © 1980 Bruce Springsteen (ASCAP). Reprinted by permission. International copyright secured. All rights reserved.

4. "The River," by Bruce Springsteen. Copyright © 1980 Bruce Springsteen (ASCAP). Reprinted by permission. International copyright secured. All rights reserved.

5. "Point Blank," by Bruce Springsteen. Copyright © 1980 Bruce Springsteen (ASCAP). Reprinted by permission. International copyright secured. All rights reserved.

Fifteen

CHEMICAL ZEN

ANDREW HUDGINS, MFA

THE LATE AFTERNOON SUN streamed in over the Pacific Ocean, brilliant, hot, and almost harsh as it angled through the sliding glass door of my father-in-law's den. My father-in-law and I had come into the room for the light. My khakis were collapsed around my white athletic shoes and ankles, and my father-in-law was sitting forward in his recliner, my limp penis and scrotum spread across his left palm, while with his left hand he fingered a tiny lump in the vessel entering my right testicle.

He was eighty-two, a retired radiologist. Yes, he said, there's definitely a lump. There's no question about that. It wasn't cancer, he was sure of that. But to put my mind at rest I should get it looked at by a urologist. He pronounced this with the insouciant certitude of someone lying to put a worried man at ease, so I didn't believe him. But after I returned home, my genitals were squeezed, pinched, and poked like a yellow crookneck squash on sale at an improbably low price. Finally my goods were ultrasounded. The urologist returned from lunch an hour late and her breath sour with wine. All the tests indicated, she said, that the lump was a benign anomaly. Nothing to worry about. How does it feel today?

It's been fine the last month," I said. "I've hardly been aware it's there. But this morning before I came into see you I squeezed it to see if it was still there and now it's throbbing a bit."

"Why don't you just leave yourself alone?" she snapped.

Imagine standing in front of a glowering inebriated woman with your pants and underwear pushed down over your hips. Your penis is still cool from her touch. She has curled her thin lips and given that pink gentleman, of whom you are shyly fond, a glance of repugnance. Imagine too that, after she has insinuated in a piercing voice that you have employed the dubious organ in some manner that is not only pernicious to your own well-being but also distasteful to her and injurious to the commonweal, you have to brush past a cowering nurse and walk through a waiting room hushed with prurient curiosity. Everyone there is trying to imagine just what enormity you have perpetrated on yourself. And so are you.

Later I found out that my father-in-law has taken my wife aside and told her I was sick too often. He was concerned about my tics, twitches, allergies, tooth grinding, acid reflux, migraines, and susceptibility to immune system problems like flu, colds, sinus attacks, infections, rashes, and shingles. He was worried that, living in a constant state of high-strung anxiety, I was wearing my system out. Sooner or later one of these problems would grab hold of me and not let go. Did I know that the shingles that had flared up on the top of my head could have spread into my eyes and blinded me? Had I thought about taking Prozac?

I'D BEEN IN COUNSELING a number of times. When I was a child my parents had been so worried about my going long weeks without saying much and then bursting into screaming fits that they took me to a psychiatrist, a blonde woman who soothed me simply by asking questions and letting me talk. Later I'd gone briefly to a counselor when I was getting divorced from my first wife, and ten years after that I began counseling again because the on-again, off-again craziness of beginning a relationship with the divorcing woman who is now my wife made me depressed, short of breath, and fragile.

The counselor I saw for ten weeks, and then with my HMO's permission for another ten, was a mousy psychology MA working a punishing schedule. With some asperity, she asked me to define any word I used that was as arcane as, well, *arcane*. She believed I was hiding my emotions behind a recondite vocabulary, one designed to make me look smart and her look stupid. She was, in fact, stupid, and I flinched when she asked me, the only time she showed any enthusiasm, if I'd read Carol Burnett's autobiography. I really should. It was a terrific book and I'd learn a lot about my life from it because Carol's dad was a lot like mine; they were both "rage-o-holics" who went off on anger binges. Still, and this is the humbling part, I am apparently a typical enough case that she didn't have to be very smart to recognize the situation I was in and how I had got there.

But counseling, for all the good it's done me, wasn't going to change a metabolism surging along a sine wave between highs of slightly giddy normality and lows where life was often an enervating chore and occasionally a welter and waste. I was a fire station in which the alarm bells seldom stopped clanging and the firemen are exhausted and indifferent. Still I resisted medication. Like a lot of artists, like a lot of *people,* I was afraid drugs would cloud my mind, my understanding, my imagination. To some extent, I'd adapted to my hummingbird nervous system and found ways to get work done and take pleasure in life. Still, the crashes were debilitating, and I was afraid they were permanently damaging my constitution. For a couple of intensely stupid months in college I had fallen in love with Nietzsche's dictum that whatever doesn't kill you makes you stronger. Well, yes, that's one thing surviving can do. But whatever doesn't kill you can still cripple you in mind, body, and spirit. Though suffering forms character and teaches us much about the world and ourselves, I doubt that my 600th day in which three or four hours are dedicated to staring at the light fixture over the bed will teach me appreciatively more than the 599th day did.

I was wary of medication because, after the breakup of my first marriage, either a berserk autoimmune response or a virus ate the myelin sheath off the nerves controlling my left arm. For four months the arm hung limply at my side, immobile from the elbow down, though I could still hold things in my hand. While admitting it probably wouldn't do any good, the doctor prescribed the standard treatment: large doses of prednisone. Over the next several months, I sniped at my girlfriend and housemate, so furious that my hands trembled and that I breathed in shallow gasps. Once, for no reason I could think of, I stood in the middle of a downtown sidewalk and blubbered in unsourced despair as people edged by me. A week later, around ten o'clock, I rose from my desk, where I'd been working calmly, went to the bathroom, and took my pill. By the time I walked back to the desk, my hands were trembling so frantically I could barely hold the pencil steady enough to write. For a long time, I sat on the floor and stared curiously at my shaking hand, looking at it as if it were something apart from me, a hairless gerbil with Parkinson's attached to the end of my wrist. The next morning, I started weaning myself off the drug and slowly, over the next month, I returned to sanity. When I mentioned it to my brother, a doctor, he said brusquely, "We call it cortisone psychosis."

Psychosis? I'd been psychotic? No, I couldn't have been psychotic, I thought, and then: Yes, psychotic—that sounds right. But try going back to the housemate you've snarled at because his twelve-pack of generic beer—white labels with nothing but the scan code on them—had impinged on your side of the top shelf of the fridge. Explain to him that it really hadn't been you picking that moronic fight—it was the drug you'd been taking. It's hard to believe your own words if you remember you've always been slightly annoyed at how, every damn morning, you'd had to shove his tumbling beer cans out of the way to get to your gallon of milk. Then go visit the woman you'd loved with frantic passion but broken up with because you'd doubted, repeatedly, her intelligence and work ethic because she was struggling with her basic statistics course. Tell her it wasn't you but the drug. Make them believe you. And that is especially hard to do if you don't really believe what you are saying because, like them, you too have clear memories of snapping out those nasty observations.

Even after the drug drained from my system and I could see I'd been acting crazily, I couldn't entirely let go of my anger, my utterly mistaken sense that these people were deliberately irritating me. The interesting thing was how similar the chemical psychosis was to the near-hysteria of anxiety in which I had lived much of my life, and how comfortably I had drifted into it, not sensing much change in how I thought or acted. I felt like a machine running beyond the limits of its approved load. In a job I held for a while after parting with my girlfriend and my housemate, I tended a sump pump beneath one of the houses my boss owned. When the sump well ran dry, I had to unplug the pump quickly or it would burn itself out trying to pump air. The gasping rackety sound it made when it ran dry, without water to slow and cool its movement, was the nerve-wracking sound of a tool destroying itself. I identified with it.

I RESISTED MY father-in-law's suggestion until about three years ago, when I was lying awake till four every morning, convinced that I was going to die of sudden acute respiratory syndrome, SARS, the virus that was trying to break out of Asia in 2002 (and died out in the fall of 2003). This way of thinking was common for me. As a child, when other boys imagined being Roman soldiers fighting for the glory of Rome I instinctively saw myself as a reluctant Visigoth forced into the ranks and killed in the first charge of the imperial phalanx, a Napoleonic conscript freezing to death on the long march back from Moscow, a Tory hanged by American patriots before the Revolutionary War started, a captured American dropping by the side and clubbed to death by rifle butts on the Bataan Death March.

Now I was again imagining an imminent death, not with terror exactly, but with a sort of fatalism. I was thinking of myself with elegiac sorrow, regretting the things I hadn't done, the things I wish I'd done better, and the years of happiness I'd miss with my wife. I was fifty-one and in good health, furious with myself for letting tabloid sensationalism get into my head. I knew the chances of contracting SARS were vanishingly minuscule, and I talked myself through the odds and the reasons behind those odds night after night, knowing I was being crazy but unable to stop, in the long hours between turning off the light for the first time and uneasy sleep, being crazy.

Finally, after my wife made me do what I had wanted but couldn't bring myself to do, I sat down with my doctor and told him about my ridiculous but unshakeable night fears. In the first month that I was on Paxil, the SSRI the doctor prescribed for me, I was so enervated that almost every afternoon I curled up in a long profound sleep, and I was so sexless that I couldn't even locate in the recesses of my mind any inclination for sex. The impulse had simply vanished. I began to see myself as a fat orange neutered tomcat, sleeping on the back of the couch in the afternoon sun—groggy, impotent, and passive to the point of being a decorative accessory in my own house.

At the same time I felt as though I could feel my mind and body calming, healing after literally a lifetime of always being at Def-Con 5. And like the nation's fifty-year-old bomber fleet, I too was experiencing metal fatigue. That's what happens when you live always expecting something bad to happen, always ready for a fight. And worse, if you are always ready to fight or flee, you end up creating trouble. You have to do something with all that martial readiness. The nasty crack you'd prepared as a defense comes out when it isn't needed, and you, thinking to deflect aggression, are now the aggressor, the one who started the squabble you'd hoped to avoid.

With the Paxil in my system, I could feel myself achieving a hint of chemical Zen, the longed-for detachment I could always see, imagine, and understand but could never achieve. I could let misunderstanding, disagreements, and jokes go by without obsessing about whether someone meant to insult me or not. At first I was concerned about the lack of sexual interest, but in time that mostly came back, if less intense than it used to be. The crucial moment came when Erin made it utterly clear that she preferred the new version of me.

Now that I was less likely to snap back at something she said, or misconstrue it, she didn't have to be so careful. She no longer worries about how I might unpredictably react if we are running late for an appointment or get lost driving in a strange part of town, or if she asks to do something at the last minute that I had not planned on. As a result, a lot of tension has slid out of her shoulders, and she can relax with me in ways she hadn't been able to do before. We've become more openly affectionate with one another, and it's been a particular and uncustomary pleasure for me to soothe her when she's blown up at her mother's imperious tone or at a student informing her that she had not properly understood his masterpiece.

HOW HAS THE MEDICATION affected me as an artist, a writer, a poet? A decade ago I was invited to visit a literature class in a prison in upstate New York, and one of the felons, a cheerful, open-faced black man asked me, "Why you so unhappy?" He meant in the poems I had read to the class—poems like this one:

ACORN

You mock us acorn scroungers.
"How the bitter nut shrivels their lips!"
you say—you eaters of milled grain,
 you who've never seen

 even the raw dough, even
the hot loaves shoveled from the oven.
You tear them and devour them,
 your soft bread alien,

 arriving with the dew.
Mock us who harvest bitter nuts,
who pound them, soak them, grind them, chew
 rough crumbling acorn bread.

 Mock us—you mock our god,
the goat god. Mock him. Have your fun.
Pass by his shrines. Neglect old gods
 with secret names, and soon

 your hogs fail even in cool weather,
your horses pull up lame, crops wither,
the hunter stumbles, women keen
 as daughters bleed obscenely.

Soon your woven robes
rot and fall from your white shoulders.
You eaters of honeyed oat cakes soon
 haunt the dark woods, and moan

 for acorns and twisted lips.
Go tell the god storms sank your ships,

ANDREW HUDGINS

your oil jar's dry, your manhood drips.
Tell him your brilliant quips.

He might reward your wit
with bitter flour flecked with grit
from shattered acorn shells. Admit
your soft souls hunger for it.

The prisoner's question was, I suppose, a version of the question every literature teacher gets—"Why are the stories and poems we read always about unhappy things? Why don't we ever read anything *cheerful?*" The usual answer is that life is serious and needs to be thought about seriously. All the cats that don't get stuck in trees that day aren't news, and neither are all the minimarts that don't get robbed. But this time I took it as a personal question: Here I am, a convicted felon, doing hard time for a long time, and there you are—clean, closely shaven, dressed in a sport coat, free to come and go. You probably own a car that's less than five years old. What's *your* problem? The guy was genuinely and genially perplexed. He really wanted to know how, with my advantages, I could be unhappy when he wasn't. I have no memory of what I said to him then, but I've come back to the question time and again in the twenty years since. In the course of the next several books I wrote, I tried to find out what makes life good when it is lived in the shadow of its own ending. What could I take pleasure in that is deeply and seriously sustaining? Sustaining, yes, but more than sustaining: nourishing. And most of all joyous, seriously joyous. There must be something beyond my previous un-understood assumption: The purpose of life is to worry.

I have tried to write about things I love—history, stories, jokes, the other, beauty, human contradiction, and love itself. A pretty obvious list, and, stated so baldly, not an interesting one. I also pondered the things I love in poetry, which I don't always love, and the answer was sound, *melopoeia,* the music of words. So I started to write more in rhyme, the old and often neglected tool that for a long time I'd found to be "fat," "superfluous," and "absurd"—to fling at it the same adjectives that Thomas Campion flung at it in 1602 in "Observations in the Art of English Poesie." Lately I have released myself, as I seldom did before, to the incantatory pleasures I'd dismissed as childish excess and frivolous preening. That's not how I regarded it in the works of the poets I admired to distraction—Hopkins, Thomas, Stevens, early Lowell, Plath, Sexton, and others. But in my own work I resolutely uprooted that kind of play, when it encroached, like weeds, into a garden as close to austere as I could make it, even in its excesses.

Besides their love of language pushed to its limits, these poets had something else in common. With the exception of Stevens, they were emotionally fragile and often disturbed. Their intense, word-driven lines sang with a high, fragile note that neared hysteria, the sentences nearing breakdown under sheer *wordness,* like glossolalia. You can hear the ecstasy they strived for, but while ecstasy means "out of the body," their language, pushed to or past the breaking point, from either pleasure or pain, sounds like it's out of its mind.

One reason I avoided too much word play was that it smacked of madness, and I came to it so easily I feared I was nuts. When I was a boy, I loved Edgar Poe because of his hysteria and madness, the shrill edge of it that permeated his lines and sentences. Like many boys, I knew the boy's version of that hysteria. I could feel in his baroque repetitions that Poe knew it deeper and with more fear, but I was also very afraid that the distance between us would not remain the gulf it was. High-strung and prone to what I wished had the poetic richness of weeping, I knew I was instead just a boy curled up crying, sometimes not knowing why he was crying and why he couldn't stop. I knew what madness sounded like. It sounded like thin metal being ground on a bench grinder, that high-pitched warbling scream of flimsy tin sheets pushed against a high-speed grinding stone. It was the sound of my nervous system. But I have learned that when you are not afraid of being obsessive, you can explore your obsessions without being swept away by them:

WAYFARERS

Wait, the wayworn
quavered. Away!
wailed the wayward,
undissuaded.
Always away!

We lay awake,
and weighed "away"
and "wait" until
away won.
Waverers
swayed, and then
still unpersuaded,

ANDREW HUDGINS

raced after us waving,
"Wait"—the way
we'd waited for.
Now eight days
along the way
into the wasteland,
our way's their way
and their way ours:
the way away.

The poets that meant the most to me were Eliot and Lowell, because I sensed great and greatly troubled minds struggling to see through their troubles, not so much to be normal as to be sane.

Shakespeare's, Pope's, and Whitman's great sanity have always drawn me to them, while I have, I am sorry to say, kept a distant and wary eye on the Romantics, other than Keats, just because they were drawn to a sentimentalized derangement of the senses that frightened and annoyed me. Now I am reading Wordsworth, Byron, and Shelley with more sympathy and patience than I could muster before, and that can only be good.

The changes in my own writing were well under way long before I began taking Paxil. I have no idea if the drug has changed my work at any fundamental level, but I doubt that it did, which is a great comfort. By toning down my anxieties, the drug has increased my ability to enjoy pleasure, to trust it instead of distrusting it. Pleasure spreads through my work in a more and more discernable way, and I have long wanted to be able to write this way. Am I then living and writing in a chemically induced illusion? I'm willing to entertain that as a theoretical question. But in all truth, I simply feel enough calmer to live a little longer than I would have done otherwise and more comfortably than I lived my first fifty-two years. Here's a poem that shows, I think, the kind of pleasures in language that I'm talking about:

THE BUTTER COW

Three-quarter ton
of sculpted butter,
the creamy Holstein's
a cold token
of its beginning.
Without a butter

bull, but under
the blue hand
of another butter
cutter, it bore,
at twenty-one,
a butter calf,
both butter mother
and butter baby
utterly butter—
from butter horn
to butter hoof,
from butter lip
to butter udder:
surplus celebrated
as surfeit and glut,
until a butcher
with a steam hose cuts
butter chop
from cutlet, chuck
from butt, and then
keeps cutting, steam
hose sputtering,
as butter lumps,
liquefying,
skitter down
the buttered gutter.

The question, of course, is how does one think about the effects of a drug with a consciousness that has been changed by the drug? If I'd suddenly begun to write very differently, I'd be more concerned than I am. If my behavior had changed in ways that those around me were clearly unhappy with, that would trouble me a lot. But my consciousness still seems wholly mine, and the things about me that had seemed crazy have ameliorated. Is something missing and I'm unable to see it? Who knows? If so, I can't discern the loss. We live our lives judging our consciousnesses with those same evolving and sometimes volatile consciousnesses, and every yardstick I know, internal and external, tells me I'm doing better. If I miss the long, compulsive streaks of writing, I do not miss the ensuing weeks of exhaustion and enervation, weeks and months when I could barely pull myself together to do my job and, at home, could only stare at books halfheartedly and moan about my inability to focus on anything but my inability to focus.

WHEN MY WIFE asked her brother what it felt like to take whatever version of Paxil he's taking, he said, "Right. I feel right for the first time in my life." I wouldn't go that far. I'm suspicious about what "right" means when we are talking about something as complex and mutable as minds. But last night after a week of mulling over how to describe my two and a half years on Paxil, I dreamed that I was standing by a window when a bomb exploded outside. For the rest of the dream, which seemed to last all night, I pulled long, jagged, onionskin-thin shards of glass out of my body. Just before I woke, I ran my hand over my body and felt my skin whole and almost smooth beneath my hand. And for the rest of the day I was distracted and tired, but I had a sense of deep accomplishment.

PSYCHOPHARMACOLOGY

AND ITS DISCONTENTS

CHASE TWICHELL, MFA

WHEN I WAS NINE OR TEN, I read a series of books by Arthur Ransome which concerned the adventures of a group of British children. One chapter opened with an epigraph from Keats:

> Or like stout Cortez when with eagle eyes
>   He star'd at the Pacific—and all his men
> Look'd at each other with a wild surmise—
>   Silent, upon a peak in Darien.

I heard it as acutely as I saw it. In four lines a world had been invented, memorialized, and left behind by a ghost, a dead poet, on a scrap of paper that could be picked up and read by me! And it made music! Nothing in my life since has fascinated me more than that portal built of words. I can still see the type in which Keats' lines were printed (letterpress, italic): "Then felt I like some watcher of the skies / When a new planet swims into his ken." Keats is spooky. His language seems to see without thinking, and he's intimate, for his language is naked—there's nothing between him and his reader, which is why the great poems last centuries.

Maybe, too, I fell in love with poetry because poets seemed to be kindred spirits: they were moody in a way I recognized. They, like me, appeared to be oddballs. I knew from an early age that I was unlike other children in some ways. My memory is, of course, partial in both senses—it's not disinterested and it's not complete—but I trust its fundamental metaphors. When I say I was half-dog, half-tomboy, cringing at the outer ring of family firelight, spying on humans, I believe that to be an accurate representation of my consciousness at ten, though just a snapshot. In every memory, I'm in the audience, not the movie, because that has always been my experience of consciousness. By ten I was well aware that being conscious of one's consciousness was not something others appeared to experience or wanted to discuss. My perception of an "I" outside the mind goes back to earliest memory. Certainly, by the time I was four or five, it was bedrock and secret. I was an Other.

As a child I was by turns turbulent and angry, sad and withdrawn. I had "bad moods," insomnia, and migraine headaches, but I was also "artistic," "creative." There was no name for what ailed me then, so I called it "unlucky," "ill-fated," "cursed," and to this day I double- and triple-check anything I buy because at least 25 percent of the time there'll be something wrong with it. (No one believes me, but it's true.) Mostly, though, I remember having "moods," which ranged from surges of excitement and energy to flashes of hell. I remember asking people what mood they were in, and being surprised when they said they hadn't thought about it. What is a "mood," anyway? Webster's says it's "a temporary state of mind or feeling." Not very helpful. In any case, mine were disordered, and back then no one had a clue how to doctor a thing like that.

My childhood was unexceptional. I was born in 1950, the eldest of three daughters, and grew up in an affluent family. My unhappily married parents fought a bitter, lifelong, covert, civilized war, without physical violence. My mother suffered from severe depression for much of my childhood. In those days, depression was thought to be the result of disturbing life experiences, so the only available relief was talk therapy. For twenty years she endured her illness without relief, while raising her children and managing a social life that included many duties that must have been exhausting for her. Having myself been depressed for extended periods of time, I'm horrified when I try to imagine what those years must have been like for her. I'm grateful to her for her courage in fighting it as hard as she did.

And, there was a Family Friend who did some Funny Business. In him I recognized neither parental authority nor affection. He smelled faintly of mothballs and knew card tricks. I was a little cowboy in a hat, standing under the hot lights with her hand on her holster. Why didn't she draw and fire? Why didn't she tell? The child cannot remember. Manners? Respect for authority? No physical injury. Embarrassment. Nothing mysterious. Besides, her parents were right upstairs, having drinks.

I saw a child psychiatrist for a year. She liked to play with naked girl and boy dolls.

From fourteen to eighteen I attended a small, repressive girls' boarding school, where my sense of social otherness was sharpened by hazing and my secret life as a poet began. I was a very poor student, scattered and unable to concentrate or memorize, much given to reading and fantasy. In the throes of adolescence, I tried on the drama of having a "gift." Great poets had one, especially if they died young. I spent many study halls writing in a red notebook, speculating about the pure need I felt to disappear into words. Was it a "calling"? Reading and trying to write poetry was thrilling, isolating, and addictive, both stimulant and narcotic. It was my first drug. I mean that quite literally. When I write, which I have done continuously ever since, I enter a state of mind in which I feel alert and slightly euphoric. My energy level rises sharply. Tea, which I have consumed in large quantities since childhood, produces a very similar state, and I so associate the two that I am unable to write without a cup of it nearby.

When I was an adolescent I smoked marijuana and found that it had a similar effect. It took me a while to figure out that, for me, the drug was not social, not relaxing. It roused in me an energy that was mental, linguistic, uncomfortable, and urgent. I wanted to be alone with paper and pen so I could write my way toward the Truth. In retrospect, I think my teenage earnestness was a fledgling form of the mind that brings postulants to the monastery and poets to the poem. *Calling* is as good a word for it as any. It's not something one would choose, but like it or not, I have it and have always had it. If it's a gift; it's one you can't give back.

When I was nineteen and struggling with my first major depression, I began to write poems that had lives of their own. That is, after a while they seemed to have been written by someone else. Many people assume, because the language of poets is unique and recognizable, that a poem's voice is that of the poet, but this is a misunderstanding. A poem's voice is a projection, a fiction invented by the poet (consciously or not) to stand in for her, to grieve and dream and kill for her, and to go on doing so long after the poet is dead. Each poem is both an artifice and an artifact of consciousness. I've come to think of poetry as a bulging warehouse (until the twentieth century it was a museum) of suffering and pleasure, joy and despair, every emotion and the full spectrum of moods, every thought and bit of logic, both ordered and disordered—it's all there, a complete history of our species' mental life to date. But we still know next to nothing about what we are, or why brain chemistry sometimes goes awry, or how to fix it.

Until I was thirty-five, I suffered periods of sometimes debilitating blues, which I presumed to be the result of repressed anger, of which I had plenty. I always managed, after a few weeks or months, to regain my equilibrium, and I was able to write two books while working at a small press and teaching at a nearby college. But when I was thirty-five I entered a terrible depression, from which I have never fully recovered. Depression is an embarrassing illness, impossible to explain to those who have never experienced it. Suffice it to say, it can be life threatening. At first I was convinced that the problem was physical. I had always had boundless energy, and suddenly I was exhausted all the time but unable to sleep. I had no appetite and lived on crackers and ginger ale. My attention span was zero. I couldn't read or even watch television without losing the thread of the story. I cried over sappy commercials. Simple tasks, like going to the grocery store or doing laundry, seemed unimaginably difficult. At the time, I was teaching in a graduate creative writing program in the South, which I came to think of as the Psycho Tropics. How I managed to teach my classes, respond to students' poems, and generally fake a normal, productive life is beyond me. Sheer will, I guess. Had I been born in an age without psychopharmaceuticals, I'd have ended up as one of those shadowy gray relatives living in someone's back bedroom.

But in 1985 there were many drugs on the market, including the dynamic duo Triavil and Elavil, first in a long parade of compounds I tried over many years, in hope and despair, searching for one that would relieve my depression without inflicting other horrors. The drugs worked. That is, they alleviated much of my physical malaise and lifted my mood to some extent. But sometimes I could barely drag myself back to consciousness in the mornings. If I stood up too quickly, I'd faint. My mouth was so dry that I had to carry a bottle of water wherever I went. My energy, on which I'd always relied, was gone. I felt slow, stupid, and lethargic, but at least I was functional. Much of that time, the Tricyclic Era, is grayed out in my memory, as if it happened far longer ago than it did. When I read them now, the poems I wrote during those years seem to yearn toward a state of mind that belongs to the past or the future, never the present. They're brainy rather than emotive, assessing rather than experiencing things directly, and their language feels somewhat willed (which of course it was). Here's an example, from "The Stolen Emblem," *Perdido*, 1991:

> It's the extinction of the thinking mind,
> the ink-dark paralysis, that terrifies,
>
> that fascinates me here, that divorces
> the self into its lonely parts.

There's a clear psychic distance between the speaker and the subject, even when the subject is the self, as in this passage lamenting its lost connection to language (from *Perdido,* "The Givens"):

I had as a child a mind
already rife with sacred greens
I could neither harvest nor ignore.
They sprang up everywhere:
from the black dirt of memory—
the old farm, its raspberries
diamonded with dew, etc.—
even from bodiless fantasy,
and from the mailbox full of letters
standing in for the various
emotions and kinds of news.

For more than twenty years I have lived and written with psychotropic drugs in my system: Triavil, Elavil, Pamelor, Desyrel, Serzone, Paxil, Zoloft, Buspar, Valium, Effexor, Xanax, Celexa, Lexapro, Wellbutrin, Seroquel, Klonopin—drugs that mercifully soothe our mental afflictions but that also alter our bodies and consciousness in a myriad of other ways, including subtly changing the way language is spoken by the mind. It's hard to explain the linguistic differences to someone who has never tinkered with his or her brain chemistry. Unlike many of the other side effects, it's not physical. Most people probably wouldn't even notice if words came to them more slowly, or if metaphors had to be hunted down rather than presenting themselves freely. But for a poet, it's crucial. For me, the most bothersome side effect of nearly every antidepressant I've taken is that my metaphor-making faculty is affected. It's as if someone has turned off the spigot. I can still make the imaginative connections and find the words eventually, but it takes longer and requires far more doggedness than it did before medications. I know this to be true because, on numerous occasions, I've tried to do without the drugs, whose other side effects can be rough. Each time the withdrawal was unbearable, but during the brief periods in which I was unmedicated, language came back to me. I remember once lying in bed, otherwise incapacitated, scribbling into a journal a pure flow of language which, when I went back to it later, made me long for the red notebook and my earlier, more direct access to words.

In my early fifties, having done some research into new drugs on the market, I fired my psychiatrist, who was incurious about them, and went in search of another. My new shrink is a genius. Unlike his predecessor, he is fascinated by psychopharmacology and knows a great deal about it while acknowledging frankly that our knowledge of mental disorders in general is primitive compared to what we know about the body. The brain is a durable mystery, a nut that remains uncracked. This doctor thought that my lifelong diagnosis of "Major Depression, recurrent" failed to account for other aspects of my mental experience, things I'd always assumed to be personal eccentricities or traits, like what friends laughingly call my "obsessions": sudden, intense, but short-lived interests: bonsai, Bob Dylan, the history of Scottish clans. Once in a while a horse would run away with me; one spring I spent several thousand dollars on eBay buying and studying marbles as the result of a sudden urgent passion to understand my father's boyhood—but mostly these infatuations were tolerated by friends and family and categorized as "harmless." Also, I seem to move faster than the average person, both physically and mentally, and in a scattered, disjointed way. I start six projects and leave them unfinished. I talk fast and interrupt myself constantly. My desk looks like a trailer park after a tornado. I work in binges rather than keep regular hours. This no doubt makes me very annoying to be around.

It's almost impossible for me to sit still. I fidget and squirm; my mind is a flock of birds. (The hardest thing I've ever attempted is zazen, the Zen practice of seated meditation. I've been doing it for fifteen years and still can't count ten breaths without my mind wandering.) I always assumed that it was my nature to be "hyper," "nervous," "speedy," "restless," "impulsive," "energetic," "impatient." It never occurred to me that these characteristics might be regarded as mental states like the blues, or anxiety—that they might be regarded as *symptoms.*

The new diagnosis was Bipolar II, categorized as a Mood Disorder, which appeared for the first time in the *Diagnostic and Statistical Manual of Mental Disorders (DSM)* only a few years ago. Ten years ago my malady had no name, and now I take three drugs for it!

Most people know that in bipolar illness, mood fluctuates between depression and mania—thus the label "manic-depression." Bipolar II labels a condition in which depression alternates with hypomania. A crucial difference between Bipolar I (manic-depression) and Bipolar II is that the latter involves *hypo*mania rather than *mania.* Unlike mania, hypomania is not psychotic, can be very subtle, and is frequently rewarded in our culture, where it goes by the names *energy, drive, ambition, perseverance, discipline,* and so forth. Hypomanic people tend to "get things done," "drive themselves at work," "go ninety miles an hour," etcetera. I had to laugh when I came across some information concerning the behavioral indicators on the American Medical Association's web site. Here's a recent self-portrait assembled entirely from language found there: *Ideas run through my head so that I cannot sleep. I'm inclined to rush from one activity to another without pausing for enough rest. I am quick in my actions. I often feel disgruntled. Ideas come and go so fast I can't keep up with them. I daydream a great deal. I often feel guilty without a very good reason for it. I am often so much on the go that sooner or later I wear myself out. I am able to work unusually long hours without feeling tired. I sometimes go on buying sprees. I frequently find myself in a meditative state. I am sometimes more talkative than usual or feel a pressure to keep talking. My feelings are hurt rather easily. I'm distractible. I'm happiest when involved in a project that calls for rapid action.* That's a pretty fair description of how I experience consciousness much of the time. (I omitted *My future often looks very dark* because I no longer feel that way, thanks to Dr. Genius.)

I now take a cocktail of three different drugs: Celexa, Wellbutrin, and Klonopin. My moods are stable and my energy plentiful. Nevertheless, I never forget that what I call my "mind" is being chemically altered on an ongoing basis. But am I less "myself" than I would otherwise be? Maybe the drugs make me *more* like my essential self, since they presumably compensate for the brain's shortcomings. So, what am I? A screwy mix of brain chemicals? Why me? Why am I compelled to write poems? Is it a blessing or a curse? (These are the same questions I was asking back in high school; I don't seem to have made a great deal of progress.)

I've gradually come to the conclusion that the Buddha was right: each of us, like the voice in a poem, is a fiction in constant flux. You're reading the words of one! Of course, that's what I've always understood poets to be: phantoms that haunt the language they leave behind. Whether it's because of the drugs I take or because I was born with a seemingly insatiable hunger to know what I am, my work as a poet and as a human being is, and has always been, to try to understand what it means to experience the world, which in my case means studying what it means to have a consciousness that appears to be unlike that of "normal" people. As a child I called it "the eyes behind the eyes." It meant I could see myself seeing, hear myself thinking. Never otherwise; I seem to have been born dissociated. In trying to perceive, articulate, and communicate what this consciousness is like, I have learned not only that it is in fact unlike others' but also that it is frequently unlike itself.

When I read back over four decades of writing, I see that I have had, and continue to have, many minds. The poems prove it. They're artifacts of the ever-changing cloud of neurons that is me. When I read my journals, which date back to early adolescence, no matter whether I was fifteen or forty, I remember those minds and the attendant emotions. But although all of them are records of what I perceived at the time to be true, the accounts frequently contradict one another. Not in terms of what happened, but in how I responded to it. This no longer surprises me. In biochemical terms, each entry was written by a unique consciousness, a stand-in for "me." An example is a note I wrote about Emily Dickinson when I was nineteen: *Negative space reversed. She sees the negative first, then calculates the positive from it. Poem = translation.* As it happens, I now understand what I meant, and think it's true of Dickinson. But scribbled in the margin next to it, in some later handwriting, are the words *pretentious crap—this means nothing*, which proves that between the time I wrote those words and now, someone else was minding the store long enough to leave a note for me.

One of the strangest things about this investigation is that no one knows exactly how most psychotropic drugs work. For that matter, we still don't know what causes affective disorders. Each edition of the *DSM* swells with new knowledge, new labels for various conditions, new speculation regarding the mysteries of the mind. For mysteries they still are, and educated guesses still the primary scaffolding of our understanding. As a poet/human/guinea pig, all I have to go on is my own experience and subjective instincts about language and how we come to a sense of self. In my most recent book, *Dog Language,* I tried to talk about it as directly as possible, poet to reader, mind to mind. Here is the poem "Neurotransmission" in its entirety:

> My history of drug-taking is long,
> starting with One-A-Day vitamins
> and St. Joseph's aspirin for children;
> pills for migraine and insomnia;
> marijuana, tea, wine;
> and then the Solaces, one by one,
> a Noah's ark of creatures too weak
> to haul away another's sorrows,
> though they lent their weight.
> Now a psychopharmacologist
> oversees the weather in my brain
> and I live in its atmospheres,
> its tides, its own distinctive
> forms of sentience.

"Life is short, art is long," said Hippocrates. "Experiment is risk, opportunity fleeting." This quotation hangs on the wall above my desk, and I try to live by its wisdom. Resurrections and transmogrifications aside, aging is the story of death. At fifty-five, I am always acutely conscious of the fleeting opportunity I have to write whatever I'm going to write. It's now or never. As a result, I think my poems have become starker, less adorned, more urgent. They have a different imaginary reader, too—someone who wants to know, as do I, what everything means, and is at the same time willing to admit that it's an unanswerable question. I understand myself to be a snake with a long history of slithering, so I'm not nearly as concerned with coming to conclusions as I once was.

Tonight, on television, the debate about Creationism raged on, and the war raged on, and as usual I stormed and sputtered and moaned. It seems to me that the world is quite crazy, quite seriously mentally ill. Kurt Vonnegut says that nature is trying to get rid of us. Isn't that obvious? Why doesn't everyone see that the world is ending? I grieve over the poor hospice we have given our earth, among ten thousand other things. Our patriotic war porn sickens me. Is our species suicidal? I'm full of despair. Is this because my brain chemistry is out of whack? The human mind is truly mysterious. A Fox News poll taken in October 2005 states that 87 percent of Americans believe in heaven, and 79 percent in angels; 74 percent believe in hell, 67 percent in the devil, 34 percent in ghosts, 24 percent in witches, and 4 percent in vampires. Psychopharmacology, it seems to me, is one of the lesser mysteries.

Now in middle age and on a mentally even keel, I am far less distressed by the way the drugs I must take affect my consciousness. I've come to love the language of our crazy culture: TV ads that tell me I should want a car with a "peppy, can-do attitude," or a character on a crime drama saying, "What?! They whacked the wrong lawyer?" Because of new media technology, the English language has gone through an astonishing, high-speed evolution in the last twenty years and shows every sign of keeping up this breakneck pace. The language we speak is the language in which we think. Our brains adapt. Why cling to archaic words? Keats wrote in the language of his time and place, and so must we. Why, too, cling to the memory of consciousness as it once was? Maybe someday I won't even remember what my "natural" mind was like. I certainly wouldn't ask for it back. As a poet, I have plenty of work to keep me busy. There are endless questions that need answers, primarily the same ones I've been asking all along.

I should go write down the stories Mom tells us over and over. We're sick of them now, but someday they'll fill us with pleasure and longing. Writing is like erasing life right as it happens. A voice speaks of its existence and then moves on.

A few days ago I was visiting an old friend, an octogenarian poet, who gave me a paper bag of Concord grapes from his yard. Their smell took me back to the grapes I used to steal from a neighbor's overgrown lot when I was a child. I was ten or eleven, and spent a lot of time playing in the abandoned garden, which had a small, locked shed full of old tools (you could see them through the window) and rickety wooden fences covered with fox grapes. One day a sign appeared on the shed door: *Private Property.* Was it because of me? Who had seen me? As a child, I considered myself invisible to adults. Had someone else been there, broken or stolen something? As I looked at the sign, I noticed that the padlock was open, so I went in. The tools were gone, and in their place was a brand new lawn mower and a red gas can. Through the dirty window I could see the tangle of weeds and trees through a scrim of spider webs. I remember that vividly—there was a dust-covered screwdriver on the sill. After that, I rarely went back there.

What does this story mean? Why did it come back to me with such specificity and vividness? I don't know, but I'm going to find out.

Richard M. Berlin, MD, physician and poet, received his undergraduate and medical education at Northwestern University. His poems have won numerous awards, and his first book of poetry, *How JFK Killed My Father,* won the Pearl Poetry Prize and was published by Pearl Editions. His poetry has also been published in a broad array of anthologies, literary journals, and medical journals, and his column, "Poetry of the Times," is featured each month in *Psychiatric Times.* An associate professor of psychiatry at the University of Massachusetts Medical School, he is the author of sixty scientific papers and is co-editor of the book *Sleep Disorders in Psychiatric Practice.* In honor of his father, he established a creative writing prize for medical students, nursing students, and resident physicians at the medical school. He practices psychiatry in a small town in the Berkshire hills of western Massachusetts.